Edited by Naomi Starkey ...y April 2013

7 **The new self**
Amy Boucher Pye *1–12 January*

20 **Praying with Psalms 50 and 51**
Ian Adams *13–26 January*

35 **Clothed in Christ**
Veronica Zundel *27 January–9 February*

50 **Jesus' wisdom in Luke (1)**
David Winter *10–23 February*

65 **Welcoming the stranger**
Michael Mitton *24 February–9 March*

80 **Jesus' wisdom in Luke (2)**
Stephen Cottrell *10–23 March*

96 **Pilgrimage through Holy Week and Easter**
Andrew Jones *24 March–6 April*

111 **The God of Jacob**
Tony Horsfall *7–20 April*

126 **Proverbs 30 and 31**
Barbara Mosse *21–30 April*

137 **The BRF Magazine**

New Daylight © BRF 2013

The Bible Reading Fellowship
15 The Chambers, Vineyard, Abingdon OX14 3FE
Tel: 01865 319700; Fax: 01865 319701
E-mail: enquiries@brf.org.uk; Website: www.brf.org.uk

ISBN 978 1 84101 758 7

Distributed in Australia by Mediacom Education Inc., PO Box 610, Unley, SA 5061.
Tel: 1800 811 311; Fax: 08 8297 8719;
E-mail: admin@mediacom.org.au
Available also from all good Christian bookshops in Australia.
For individual and group subscriptions in Australia:
Mrs Rosemary Morrall, PO Box W35, Wanniassa, ACT 2903.

Distributed in New Zealand by Scripture Union Wholesale, PO Box 760, Wellington
Tel: 04 385 0421; Fax: 04 384 3990; E-mail: suwholesale@clear.net.nz

Publications distributed to more than 60 countries

Acknowledgments

Printed in Singapore by Craft Print International Ltd

Suggestions for using *New Daylight*

Find a regular time and place, if possible, where you can read and pray undisturbed. Before you begin, take time to be still and perhaps use the BRF prayer. Then read the Bible passage slowly (try reading it aloud if you find it over-familiar), followed by the comment. You can also use *New Daylight* for group study and discussion, if you prefer.

The prayer or point for reflection can be a starting point for your own meditation and prayer. Many people like to keep a journal to record their thoughts about a Bible passage and items for prayer. In *New Daylight* we also note the Sundays and some special festivals from the Church calendar, to keep in step with the Christian year.

New Daylight and the Bible

New Daylight contributors use a range of Bible versions, and you will find a list of the versions used opposite, on page 2. You are welcome to use your own preferred version alongside the passage printed in the notes, and this can be particularly helpful if the Bible text has been abridged.

New Daylight affirms that the whole of the Bible is God's revelation to us, and we should read, reflect on and learn from every part of both Old and New Testaments. Usually the printed comment presents a straight-forward 'thought for the day', but sometimes it may also raise questions rather than simply providing answers, as we wrestle with some of the more difficult passages of Scripture.

New Daylight *is also available in a deluxe edition (larger format). Check out your local Christian bookshop or contact the BRF office, who can also give more details about a cassette version for the visually impaired. For a Braille edition, contact St John's Guild, 8 St Raphael's Court, Avenue Road, St Albans, AL1 3EH.*

Writers in this issue

Amy Boucher Pye is an American who has lived in the UK for over a decade. She makes her home in North London with her husband and young family and enjoys writing for Christian periodicals, including *Quiet Spaces*, *Woman Alive* and *Christian Marketplace*.

Ian Adams is an Anglican priest, writer, poet, teacher and artist working with themes of spirituality, prayer, culture and community. He is the author of *Cave Refectory Road* (Canterbury Press, 2010). He is also a director of the StillPoint project (thestillpoint.org.uk).

Veronica Zundel is an Oxford graduate, writer and journalist. She lives with her husband and son in North London, where they belong to the Mennonite Church.

David Winter is retired from parish ministry. An honorary Canon of Christ Church, Oxford, he is well known as a writer and broadcaster. His most recent book for BRF is *Facing the Darkness and Finding the Light*.

Michael Mitton is a freelance writer, speaker and consultant and the Fresh Expressions Adviser for the Derby Diocese. He is also the NSM Priest-in-charge of St Paul's Derby and honorary Canon of Derby Cathedral. He is the author of *Dreaming of Home* (BRF 2012).

Stephen Cottrell is the Bishop of Chelmsford. He has worked as Missioner in the Wakefield diocese and as part of Springboard, the Archbishop's evangelism team. His latest books are *From the Abundance of the Heart* (DLT, 2006) and *Do Nothing to Change Your Life* (CHP, 2007).

Andrew Jones is Archdeacon of Meirionnydd in the Diocese of Bangor and rector of four churches on the Llyn Peninsula in North Wales. He has led many pilgrimages in the UK and abroad and has also written *Pilgrimage: the journey to remembering our story* (BRF, 2011).

Tony Horsfall is a freelance trainer and retreat leader based in Yorkshire, with his own ministry, Charis Training. He is an elder of Ackworth Community Church and has written several books for BRF, including *Working from a Place of Rest* and *Servant Ministry* (available March 2013).

Barbara Mosse is an Anglican priest with experience in prison, university, community mental health and hospital chaplaincies. She is the author of *The Treasures of Darkness* (Canterbury Press, 2003) and *Encircling the Christian Year* (BRF, 2012).

Naomi Starkey writes...

Wisdom is an attribute that tends not to be widely celebrated in today's world. Stories of talent (especially of the performing arts variety), cleverness (especially of the passing exams variety) and cunning (especially of the political 'spin' variety) are what so often dominate the media. Wisdom, on the other hand, may be far less showy, far more of a back-stage, behind-the-scenes kind of influence—but one that, if heeded, has the potential to transform a situation or relationship.

Over this coming year, *New Daylight* includes an extended series of readings exploring the theme of Jesus' wisdom, as found in Luke's Gospel. David Winter and Stephen Cottrell have written two weeks each in this issue and, as David puts it in his introduction: 'This wisdom... is more than intelligence or knowledge—insight, vision and understanding are its roots.' I hope you find much food for thought as you follow the series; I have certainly gained a lot from editing it.

I would also like to welcome a new contributor, Ian Adams, who guides us prayerfully through Psalms 50 and 51. His notes are followed by a very different topic: clothing and hair in the Bible! Far from being a frivolous diversion, however, this topic raises important questions to do with how we interpret scripture, especially in relation to everyday life. Veronica Zundel offers stimulating insights to help us in this challenging process.

Our Holy Week and Easter readings are brought to us by Andrew Jones, who invites us to accompany him on an imaginative pilgrimage to some of the places most closely linked to the events of this special season in the Church's calendar. Andrew writes from many years' experience as a pilgrimage leader, both in the UK and abroad, as well as time spent studying in Israel. His readings are a vivid reminder that the events we commemorate happened in real places, at a specific time in history. We may not have had (or ever hope to have) the privilege of visiting the actual sites, but this Easter we can travel there in our hearts and, like any pilgrims, journey onward with renewed energy and God-given hope.

The BRF Prayer

Almighty God,
you have taught us that your word is a lamp for our feet
and a light for our path. Help us, and all who prayerfully
read your word, to deepen our fellowship with you
and with each other through your love.
And in so doing may we come to know you more fully,
love you more truly, and follow more faithfully
in the steps of your son Jesus Christ, who lives and reigns
with you and the Holy Spirit, one God for evermore.
Amen

The new self

January strikes a cold note in the hearts of many. After the excesses of December, with its celebrations and feasts, the new year dawns and we may wonder if we would rather just stay under the duvet. We drag ourselves to what in an image-obsessed culture might be the ultimate reality check—the scales—and see what sort of havoc our overindulgence has wreaked. 'It's time for new resolutions!' we cry, horrified at the number appearing below us.

Our Bible passages to start 2013 fit well with new beginnings, for we will examine the theme of our old and new selves—how, at conversion, we leave behind the old and embrace the new identity that is being formed in Christ. Of course, we could explore this theme at any time of the year, for the new birth is foundational to our lives as redeemed people, but looking at it now may help us to infuse any New Year's resolutions with the riches of spiritual depth we find in the Bible. As we shed the old self and put on the new, living empowered by the triune God, we are able to leave behind our former ways of life—perhaps those invaded by bitterness, anger, hurt or rage. When we put on our new self, our lives will show forth the fruits of the Spirit—love, joy, peace, patience, kindness, goodness, faithfulness, gentleness and self-control.

The passages that follow come from the Old Testament and the New, starting at the beginning in the garden of Eden, where the choices of our first parents effected the need for a new Adam—namely, Jesus Christ. We move through some of the prophets and see how they called the Israelites to have a new name and a new heart. Then we engage with Jesus and the teachings of the early Church. The apostle Paul, especially, writes on the new birth and life that we can enjoy after we submit ourselves to God. He, who was changed so radically on the road to Damascus, writes with a passion and urgency that exceeds any bland New Year's resolution. If we put to death what used to cling to our earthly nature, we will move forward in the freedom of light and life.

Amy Boucher Pye

Dead in Adam; alive in Christ

'You will not certainly die', the serpent said to the woman. 'For God knows that when you eat from it your eyes will be opened, and you will be like God, knowing good and evil.' When the woman saw that the fruit of the tree was good for food and pleasing to the eye, and also desirable for gaining wisdom, she took some and ate it. She also gave some to her husband, who was with her, and he ate it. Then the eyes of both of them were opened, and they realised they were naked.

As I deliberated about where to start our thematic look at old self/new self, I realised the obvious—that our best jumping-off point is at the fall of humanity, for there, in the garden of Eden, we first experienced the need for a new self. When Adam and Eve disobeyed God's instructions, instead following the serpent's tempting invitation to come and eat, they introduced sin into the world and into our hearts. No longer would we walk freely, without shame. Now men would be governed by the need to work and women would pine for their husbands.

Thankfully, the triune God, in his graciousness, does not leave us in the garden, hopeless and helpless. He covers their (and our) shame not only practically—with garments of skin (see v. 21)—but also spiritually through Jesus' death on the cross. We are born fallen, as a result of the effects of our first parents' disobedience, but we can be redeemed by the new Adam, who was the perfect sacrifice. As Paul said in his first letter to the Corinthians, 'For as in Adam all die, so in Christ all will be made alive' (1 Corinthians 15:22).

We may be making resolutions today as we embark on 2013, but let's remember that true and lasting change comes from living in Christ. As he dwells in us through his Holy Spirit, he will help us to leave behind our sinful patterns of behaviour and travel a more fruitful path of new life.

Prayer

Father, Son and Holy Spirit, we dedicate our lives in 2013 to your glory. Help us to shed the old and embrace the new.

AMY BOUCHER PYE

One or the other?

When pride comes, then comes disgrace, but with humility comes wisdom… Whoever derides their neighbour has no sense, but the one who has understanding holds their tongue. A gossip betrays a confidence, but a trustworthy person keeps a secret… A wicked person earns deceptive wages, but the one who sows righteousness reaps a sure reward. Truly the righteous attain life, but whoever pursues evil finds death… A generous person will prosper; whoever refreshes others will be refreshed… Whoever brings ruin on their family will inherit only wind, and the fool will be servant to the wise.

In this chapter of Proverbs, the sage gives a contrasting picture of the wicked and the wise. The former fall into pride and disgrace, while the latter find refreshment and righteousness. Those who seek evil will experience ruin, deception, betrayal and ultimately death, whereas the righteous will be humble, prosperous and find life.

Reading about these pairings of opposites can lead us to think that we are inevitably one or the other—wicked or wise. We can despair that we will always be beholden to our sinful nature and will never find victory over temptation or addictions. Alternatively, we can puff ourselves up, thinking with pride that we have this spiritual life sussed and conquered—we have arrived. The truth, however, probably lies in the tension of the 'already but not yet'. As Christians, we have been redeemed by Jesus' sacrifice, but we are not yet fully transformed. We still fall into sinful patterns of behaving. Yet, as we live empowered by the Holy Spirit, we can enjoy more freedom and more grace to become increasingly like the righteous people we see in these proverbs.

Humility; holding one's tongue; wisdom; keeping confidences; sowing righteousness; pursuing life; displaying generosity; bringing refreshment… all characteristics of the new self. Why not join me in asking God to help us live out these qualities this day, this month and this year?

Prayer

Triune God, I know that on my own I quickly fall into patterns of the old self. Come and live in and through me, that I might reveal your love, generosity and grace to those whom I meet.

AMY BOUCHER PYE

A royal diadem

The nations will see your vindication, and all kings your glory; you will be called by a new name that the mouth of the Lord will bestow. You will be a crown of splendour in the Lord's hand, a royal diadem in the hand of your God. No longer will they call you Deserted, or name your land Desolate. But you will be called Hephzibah, and your land Beulah; for the Lord will take delight in you, and your land will be married. As a young man marries a young woman, so will your Builder marry you; as a bridegroom rejoices over his bride, so will your God rejoice over you.

We might feel uncomfortable applying the language of the prophet Isaiah to our lives—men in particular might struggle with calling themselves a royal diadem or the bride of Christ—but, to paraphrase what C.S. Lewis once wrote, God is so masculine that we are all feminine in response to him. So it is that, male or female, we can ask God to reveal how his loving words from centuries ago can speak into our spirits and souls today.

Being a crown of splendour in the Lord's hand makes me think of Jesus on the cross, wearing his crown of thorns. He who could take the place of the righteous king chose to endure pain for our sakes so that we, too, can be sons and daughters of the king, wearing a jewel-encrusted crown as bestowed by our heavenly Father.

No longer do we have to endure desolate lives of emptiness, for God reassures his people that he dwells with us and delights in us. He who has created us—the Builder—who has set our foundations into place, will rejoice over us even as a bridegroom on his wedding day.

Living out of the new self entails embracing our identity as the beloved. Our new name reflects joy, rejoicing, delight and love. What name could you claim today?

Reflection

'"Come, I will show you the bride, the wife of the Lamb"… It shone with the glory of God, and its brilliance was like that of a very precious jewel, like a jasper, clear as crystal' (Revelation 21:9, 11).

AMY BOUCHER PYE

Discordant music

My people come to you, as they usually do, and sit before you to hear your words, but they do not put them into practice. Their mouths speak of love, but their hearts are greedy for unjust gain. Indeed, to them you are nothing more than one who sings love songs with a beautiful voice and plays an instrument well, for they hear your words but do not put them into practice.

The prophet Ezekiel wrote after the fall of Jerusalem, when the Jewish people were exiled to Babylon. The unthinkable happened and no longer could they worship in the temple or live in their familiar city. In their anguish, they must have wondered if the Lord had abandoned them, but they also allowed their pain to create a growing distance from God. They became complacent and removed from the cares of the Lord.

The Lord tells Ezekiel that his prophecies are not penetrating the hearts of his people; the words only waft above them like beautiful but meaningless music. Greed hides under their proclamations of love. Their spiritual state sounds similar to that of the people of the church at Sardis, to whom Jesus wrote through the apostle John—'I know your deeds; you have a reputation of being alive, but you are dead. Wake up!' (Revelation 3:1–2)—or, indeed, those of the church at Laodicea, whom he called lukewarm (v. 16).

Sloughing off the old self and living out of the new entails our whole lives. A baby bird grows stronger and surer of itself as it pecks through and emerges from its shell. So too will we gain spiritual weight and wisdom as we dedicate our everything to the Lord—our thoughts, words and actions. Whatever stage of life we are in, whether we are in the process of breaking through the shell or soaring through the air with fully developed wings, may we lean on God as our source of everlasting strength and hope.

Prayer

Lord Jesus, like the disciples in the garden of Gethsemane, we struggle to stay awake. Stir us up, we pray, so that we do not become smug spiritually or unconcerned for the world around us.

AMY BOUCHER PYE

A new heart and a new spirit

'It is not for your sake, people of Israel, that I am going to do these things, but for the sake of my holy name, which you have profaned among the nations where you have gone... I will sprinkle clean water on you, and you will be clean; I will cleanse you from all your impurities and from all your idols. I will give you a new heart and put a new spirit in you; I will remove from you your heart of stone and give you a heart of flesh. And I will put my Spirit in you and move you to follow my decrees and be careful to keep my laws.'

We might think that the Holy Spirit is absent in the Old Testament, but he is definitely present—if sometimes hidden. Here God says that he will give his Holy Spirit to his people, to live and move among them and to lead them to holiness.

In Ezekiel's words, we see turning from the old self to the new as a process of conversion. First, there is an outward cleansing (purification); second, there is a heart transplant (renovation); third, there is a filling with the Holy Spirit and the right living that results (sanctification). Of course, people will have different experiences of coming to faith in the triune God, but these steps reveal the level of transformation it entails. God changes our hearts and our spirits, which, according to Hebrew understanding, meant not just our emotions but also our wills.

Why does God go to these lengths to restore his fallen people? It is for his glory, because his name was being profaned as they lived outside of the promised land. As the neighbouring nations witness God saving his people, they will realise his power and grace.

A 'heart of stone' is cold, lifeless, often bitter. The Lord wants to remove any pebbles or rocks that lodge in our hearts, so that his Spirit might flow through us. Heart surgery is painful, but, as God unclogs our arteries and cleans out any built-up muck, we reap physical, emotional and spiritual rewards.

Reflection

'*Create in me a pure heart, O God, and renew a steadfast spirit within me*'
(*Psalm 51:10*).

Amy Boucher Pye

John 3:4–8 (NIV)

Born again

'How can someone be born when they are old?' Nicodemus asked. 'Surely they cannot enter a second time into their mother's womb to be born!' Jesus answered, 'Very truly I tell you, no one can enter the kingdom of God unless they are born of water and the Spirit. Flesh gives birth to flesh, but the Spirit gives birth to spirit. You should not be surprised at my saying, "You must be born again." The wind blows wherever it pleases. You hear its sound, but you cannot tell where it comes from or where it is going. So it is with everyone born of the Spirit.'

An older friend of mine speaks freely of being 'born again' to those whom she meets—shop assistants, taxi drivers, professional contacts. Part of me cringes when she employs this language, as the phrase has fallen out of fashion, even become tainted, bringing up images of overly zealous fundamentalist Christians shouting, 'Ye must be born again'!

I shouldn't be embarrassed, though, for the source of the words is Jesus. When Nicodemus, a Pharisee who was on the Jewish ruling council, converses with Jesus, he seems to be taking Jesus literally and not understanding the role of the Spirit in birthing a new person. We might not be able to see the Spirit physically, as perhaps Nicodemus was trying to do, but we will witness its evidence in our lives and in the lives of others—as we witness the wind blowing through the trees.

John does not tell us here if Nicodemus was born of the Spirit (later we learn that he joined Joseph of Arimathea to bury Jesus' body, so we can guess that his earlier encounter brought life). Instead, John moves on to some of the most famous verses in the Bible, about God so loving the world that he gave his one and only Son (3:16)… Our new birth comes from the transforming work of God through Jesus on the cross, so that we might escape condemnation and enter the light.

Prayer
Heavenly Father, we do not fully understand how your Spirit works in our lives. Reveal to us your transforming nature, that we might know and believe.

Amy Boucher Pye

Slaves to righteousness

But thanks be to God that, though you used to be slaves to sin, you have come to obey from your heart the pattern of teaching that has now claimed your allegiance. You have been set free from sin and have become slaves to righteousness. I am using an example from everyday life because of your human limitations. Just as you used to offer yourselves as slaves to impurity and to ever-increasing wickedness, so now offer yourselves as slaves to righteousness leading to holiness... But now that you have been set free from sin and have become slaves of God, the benefit you reap leads to holiness, and the result is eternal life.

The theme of leaving behind the old self and embracing the new shines through the letters of Paul. Of course, this follows from his dramatic conversion. One moment he was persecuting Christians to the point of death; the next he was rendered blind as Jesus revealed himself to him, changing his life (and the world) forever.

As we see in today's passage, the new life does not happen automatically. Our wills need to be involved and committed. Paul employs the example of slavery, showing how we need to offer ourselves—our minds, hearts, emotions, actions—to right living before God. This then produces purity, holiness and eternal life.

I recently heard an illustration that warns against our temptation to entertain sin. An eagle sees a fresh carcass floating on some ice, but moving towards a waterfall. The ice provides the eagle a place to land and from which to pick at the carcass. As the waterfall approaches, the eagle sneaks in just a few more bites, but, when it tries to lift off, it finds its claws are frozen into the ice and it falls to its death. Now, I am not suggesting that we are heading for that waterfall! As Paul says, because we have become slaves to God, we will have eternal life—but the eagle can be a vivid cautionary tale against living out of the old self.

Reflection

'Therefore, if anyone is in Christ, the new creation has come: the old has gone, the new is here!' (2 Corinthians 5:17).

AMY BOUCHER PYE

2 Corinthians 5:1–5 (NIV)

An eternal perspective

For we know that if the earthly tent we live in is destroyed, we have a building from God, an eternal house in heaven, not built by human hands. Meanwhile we groan, longing to be clothed instead with our heavenly dwelling, because when we are clothed, we will not be found naked. For while we are in this tent, we groan and are burdened, because we do not wish to be unclothed but to be clothed instead with our heavenly dwelling, so that what is mortal may be swallowed up by life. Now the one who has fashioned us for this very purpose is God, who has given us the Spirit as a deposit, guaranteeing what is to come.

I ended our yearly Christmas missive one year with a reflection on the fragility of life, as someone close to us was killed in a car accident. I did not know that, as I composed the letter, a beloved older friend was near death, having suffered a stroke. We often live in a state of denial, but, for everyone, one day the 'earthly tent' will be destroyed.

Yet Paul here speaks to the Corinthians about longing for his heavenly dwelling, which God the Builder and Architect has created and moths and rust will not destroy. It is another variation of the 'already, not yet' state we are in, mentioned earlier. That is, we have been redeemed, but are not yet completely sanctified. Here, we note that we groan on earth as we anticipate the wonders of heaven—namely, our rich communion with God.

I love the way Paul reverses the wisdom of the world with his phrase, 'swallowed up by life' (in contrast to death being the great swallower). All the remnants of our old selves—the mortal—will be swallowed up by the true and everlasting light and life in our heavenly dwelling. We will no longer be naked and ashamed, but clothed in a better outfit than we ever could have dreamed of.

Prayer

Lord God, help me to live with an eternal perspective today, remembering that people and your word will be all that remains eternally. Plant in me the hope of heaven, which you promise will not disappoint.

AMY BOUCHER PYE

New clothes

> You were taught, with regard to your former way of life, to put off your old self, which is being corrupted by its deceitful desires; to be made new in the attitude of your minds; and to put on the new self, created to be like God in true righteousness and holiness.

I used to have a white jumper that I called my 'travelling sweater'. For some reason, I considered it the best and most comfortable item of clothing to wear on an aeroplane, but, after many a journey, it became slightly grey and shapeless, sporting some holes. Still, I loved it—so much that my mother and sister had to recommend I finally retire my favourite travel companion.

Putting off the old self and putting on the new can feel like leaving behind a familiar way of life. Even if the former way of life leads to pain, heartache, angst, anger and destruction, we fear what we might encounter in the new. Will we have fun? Will we be fulfilled? What will we have to give up?

As we don our new clothes in Christ, our minds and hearts are made new. We begin to see how misshapen our old clothes were; how tight they felt and how we could not breathe in them. The trousers, in fact, gave us indigestion. Our new clothes not only reveal who we really are but also enable us to soar in freedom, truth and holiness.

In what might be the clearest passage about the old and new selves, Paul points out three imperatives: put off your old self; be made new in your mind; put on the new self. Elsewhere, he speaks of living 'in Christ', which gives us the power and strength to live out these imperatives. As we do so, we will be 'created to be like God', which hearkens back to the Genesis account of creation. Through our continued donning of the new self, we can live as God intended, with right living and holiness.

Prayer

Lord Jesus, help me to cast off any clothing of the past that I need to leave behind. Renew my mind that I might put on my new self.

AMY BOUCHER PYE

Give thanks

We continually ask God to fill you with the knowledge of his will through all the wisdom and understanding that the Spirit gives, so that you may live a life worthy of the Lord and please him in every way: bearing fruit in every good work, growing in the knowledge of God, being strengthened with all power according to his glorious might so that you may have great endurance and patience, and giving joyful thanks to the Father, who has qualified you to share in the inheritance of his holy people in the kingdom of light. For he has rescued us from the dominion of darkness and brought us into the kingdom of the Son he loves, in whom we have redemption, the forgiveness of sins.

A primary characteristic of the new life is a spirit of thankfulness. Here, Paul and Timothy are writing to the church at Colossae and, in these opening verses, they pray that the believers will live out their new life. This is not only so that they might be strengthened to endure and be patient but also all the while 'giving joyful thanks to the Father'.

In the West today we so easily see what we are missing, especially when advertising slogans continually reassure that 'you're worth it'. We might pine after physical things, such as the latest mobile phone or laptop. We may pine in our relationships—longing to be married, to have a baby, for our children to find fulfilment and so on. Yet, when we stop and ponder all that we have, our outlook changes. We begin to wonder at the treasures we have already received. Our senses become open to beauty, even if it is just hearing the birdsong in a concrete jungle.

Some poets and philosophers see thanksgiving as an overriding virtue. For instance, G.K. Chesterton said in *A Short History of England* (1917), 'I would maintain that thanks are the highest form of thought, and that gratitude is happiness doubled by wonder'. Good advice for the new life.

Prayer

Triune God, change my spirit that I might give thanks in all things. Let me know how you pour out your love and mercy on me, making me clean.

AMY BOUCHER PYE

Destroying walls

Do not lie to each other, since you have taken off your old self with its practices and have put on the new self, which is being renewed in knowledge in the image of its Creator. Here there is no Gentile or Jew, circumcised or uncircumcised, barbarian, Scythian, slave or free, but Christ is all, and is in all. Therefore, as God's chosen people, holy and dearly loved, clothe yourselves with compassion, kindness, humility, gentleness and patience. Bear with each other and forgive one another if any of you has a grievance against someone. Forgive as the Lord forgave you. And over all these virtues put on love, which binds them all together in perfect unity.

Sadly, often in church life we fight battles with each other—brothers and sisters against brothers and sisters. Perhaps we deem that we hold the whole truth and they fall short. Maybe a difference of opinion over a point of doctrine becomes the opening clash of a long and drawn-out war, which leaves lives bruised and relationships impaired.

As the wife of a vicar, I have witnessed such spats between siblings. I do not count myself as an authority on conflict resolution, nor do I claim to hold an infallible grasp on truth, but we see a way forward in our church family's life through Paul's letter to the Colossians. As we live out our redeemed lives, Christ is all and is in all.

We can take off the old clothes, to employ again that metaphor for the new self, and put on the clothes of Christ—compassion, kindness, humility, gentleness, patience, forgiveness, love. Wearing his garments, we are more able to live in harmony and peace with our fellows, especially if we remember that Christ's sacrifice for us is that which he made for them. We can then hope to move forward in unity, being freed from infighting as we seek to love others and love God.

Reflection

'And let us consider how we may spur one another on towards love and good deeds. Let us not give up meeting together, as some are in the habit of doing, but let us encourage one another—and all the more as you see the Day approaching' (Hebrews 10:24–25).

AMY BOUCHER PYE

A new name

Whoever has ears, let them hear what the Spirit says to the churches. To the one who is victorious, I will give some of the hidden manna. I will also give that person a white stone with a new name written on it, known only to the one who receives it.

A couple of women I know have changed their given names. One suffered sexual abuse and, by changing her name, she was cutting painful ties. Another did not want to be defined by her name's meaning, which was 'bitter'. Instead, she wanted to be known by a name that denotes 'grace'.

Our passage comes from the letters of Jesus, as revealed to the ageing apostle John. Jesus says to the church at Pergamum that he will give them a white stone with a new name on it, known only to the recipient. Several meanings of this white stone have been put forward, as summarised by Craig Keener in the *NIV Application Commentary: Revelation* (pp. 126–27). One is that, in the ancient world, people used pebbles for admission to events—in this case, to a messianic banquet. Another is that, in some ancient courtrooms, the jurors would cast a white stone for acquittal or a black one for conviction. (Thus, Jesus would be the judge over what the Pergamum Christians were suffering.) The white stone could also symbolise purity and eternal life or a new name, signifying a new identity.

The symbolic possibilities are rich. Applying the promise to our own lives hearkens back to the promises we examined in Isaiah 62 on 3 January. Our new name might be one that we publicise as we embrace our new, redeemed self or it might be one that we keep hidden—the name that we hear when we call to the Lord and listen for his affirming words of love.

We are no longer bound to the old way of life. As we live out of our new selves in 2013, may we reflect the attributes of the one who created us, who made us for himself.

Reflection

'Let us rejoice and be glad and give him glory! For the wedding of the Lamb has come, and his bride has made herself ready' (Revelation 19:7).

AMY BOUCHER PYE

Praying with Psalms 50 and 51

The psalms always take us into the nature of human being at its most real and earthy. Life is a compelling mix of sinning and shining. It is this combination that will be up front and centre in this series of readings.

Sacrifice and sin are the demanding themes that confront us in Psalms 50 and 51. Psalm 50 focuses on what might or might not be an acceptable sacrifice to God. Psalm 51 is the psalm that David famously composed after the revelation of his adultery with Bathsheba and his murderous manipulation of her husband, Uriah the Hittite.

These psalms ask difficult questions, such as 'Is God really pleased or appeased by our sacrifices?' As we will see, the psalms hint that he is not—but the psalmist can never quite let the idea go. Is sin our defining characteristic from birth or is there another option, possibly bringing more hope, for how we might view and define ourselves?

Our response to these questions will lead us to ask further demanding questions of ourselves and the text. How do we live with parts of the Bible that we find difficult, jarring or even distasteful? To what extent do we allow our contemporary sensibilities to sway the way that we engage with scripture?

We will explore some of the tensions involved in holding scripture as being, on the one hand, a collection of texts written in different ways by different people with different aims in different times and, on the other hand, still holding it as *one* or even *the* primary source of God-breathed wisdom, learning and presence. We will also wonder if the best prism for viewing these ancient writings might be the life and teachings of Jesus, as told in the Gospels and mused on in the rest of the New Testament.

Lent is not far off—a traditional time for self-examination, clearing the decks, preparing ourselves to follow Jesus the Christ through the descent of his Passion and the ascent of his resurrection. So, perhaps this is a really good time to be thinking, praying and working through these issues, and to reflect on our sinning and shining. Peace to you.

Ian Adams

The sun rises: a new day

The mighty one, God the Lord, speaks and summons the earth from the rising of the sun to its setting. Out of Zion, the perfection of beauty, God shines forth.

The sun rises: a new day. It is not yet the middle of January, so, depending on where you are and the state of the weather when you are reading this, the dawn light may be brilliant or it may be hard to see. Either way, it is happening, wonderfully, beautifully and full of promise.

The opening to Psalm 50 sets the scene for everything that follows. It reminds us of how God is always creating, re-creating and sustaining all of creation. It reminds us how beautiful this creation is. It also reminds us how this amazing world exudes the beauty and wonder of God. 'God shines forth' from the world around us, from our neighbour and from the stranger and, wonderfully, also from you and me.

The opening of this psalm also resonates with sounds from elsewhere in scripture. In imagining that God 'speaks and summons' the new day into glorious being, the psalm is listening back deep into Jewish tradition. It is picking up an echo from the great creation story told in Genesis, where new life is spoken into existence, with each new movement of creation unfolding to the phrase 'And God said…'.

The psalm also hints that we may look forward. On this day, much of the Church celebrates the baptism of Christ—the starting point for the public ministry of Jesus. The baptism is announced by the voice of the Father summoning the earth and its people to see the new thing that is coming into being (Matthew 3:17). Also, of course, in the amazing prologue to John's Gospel, the Christ who sustains creation is himself spoken of as 'the Word'. So, as we read Psalm 50, we are immersing ourselves in a great tradition that stretches backwards and forwards.

Reflection

The sun rises: it is a new day. If you can, take a walk outside. Pay attention to the beauty of the created world around you. Look for signs of God 'shining forth' and notice what this produces in you.

IAN ADAMS

Pause, ponder

Our God comes and does not keep silence, before him is a devouring fire, and a mighty tempest all around him. He calls to the heavens above and to the earth, that he may judge his people: 'Gather to me my faithful ones, who made a covenant with me by sacrifice!' The heavens declare his righteousness, for God himself is judge. *Selah*

Pause. Take a moment. Ponder.

The psalmist includes a single but vital word of instruction in this part of Psalm 50, a word that is easy to ignore or miss altogether. The word 'selah' seems to be an instruction to pause, to take a moment, to ponder. How important this is—but how difficult it can seem to carve out the space and the time to do this consistently. So, here I do not want to just give you yet more words, but space for 'selah'.

The context for this instruction to pause is the declaration that God does come among us and does speak. Our experience may be that, much of the time, God seems to be relatively silent, but the contemplatives tell us that God comes in humility; God is never forced upon us. The psalmist is also insistent that, whatever our perception, God is not far off.

In this passage, the powerful presence of God is sensed in a storm resounding with thunder and lightning. Like a judge making a righteous decision in court that will bring justice for everyone, this is how God's 'making everything right' will happen. It will ring out with great clarity and the injustices that must, at this time, be borne in silence will be put right. The inequalities that mar society will be remedied. The promises that have been broken will be restored.

So, pause. Take a moment. Ponder. What are the injustices that you face? What might be the inequalities that concern you? Are there broken promises that are damaging us and those around us?

Prayer
God of righteousness, help me to pause and so sense your joyful, restoring, presence. Bring your justice and peace to the world, to the people I care for, to places where I belong and to me.

IAN ADAMS

22

What do you want from me?

'Hear, O my people, and I will speak, O Israel, I will testify against you. I am God, your God. Not for your sacrifices do I rebuke you; your burnt offerings are continually before me. I will not accept a bull from your house, or goats from your folds. For every wild animal of the forest is mine, the cattle on a thousand hills. I know all the birds of the air, and all that moves in the field is mine.'

This part of Psalm 50 seems to lead to a question: 'What do you want from me?'—specifically, 'God, what do you want from me?' In the spirit of yesterday's reading, it is worth making a 'selah' space here, too. Pause, take a moment, ponder and ask, 'God, what do you want from me?'

Most of us have, to some extent, a desire to please others. Our motives will be mixed, of course—but that's life, that's us, and it's fine. We may need to be liked, we may thrive on approval or we may genuinely want to bring happiness to others. Probably, something of each of these impulses will be present in the mix.

The sociological and religious roots that helped shape the faith story of the psalmist's people included a widespread belief in the importance and efficacy of sacrifice. The god(s), the story went, would be appeased and pleased by some kind of offering or sacrifice. Sacrifice was at the heart of God's covenant with Israel, too. This may seem primitive and even distasteful to us now, so what can do we do with this emphasis on sacrifice?

It is interesting that in this passage and the accompanying section we will work with tomorrow, there is more than a hint that sacrifice is not actually what God wants from us—certainly not the sacrifice of animals. Perhaps more relevantly, there is a sense that God cannot be bargained with or 'bought off'. God may want something much more interesting from us...

Reflection

Let our question become a prayer, but do not forecast the answer.
Ask the question, then fall into silence. Let the question be,
'God, what do you want from me?'

IAN ADAMS

As simple as 'thank you'

'If I were hungry, I would not tell you, for the world and all that is in it is mine. Do I eat the flesh of bulls, or drink the blood of goats? Offer to God a sacrifice of thanksgiving, and pay your vows to the Most High. Call on me in the day of trouble; I will deliver you, and you shall glorify me.'

It may be as simple as 'thank you'. If—as the psalmist seems to be saying here—God is less than impressed by sacrifice, what might be wanted of us? It may feel like a cliché, but there's no doubt that one of the many things that keeps the world going round is the giving of thanks.

At its best, thanksgiving is not offered as a way of seeking (further) favour. Rather, thanksgiving is a genuine sign of appreciation that honours the one(s) being thanked. At its best, too, thanksgiving is not received as an expected reward, but accepted as an authentic gesture of gratitude. When given and received in this spirit, thanksgiving can become a blessing to both giver and receiver. The act of thanksgiving connects us with each other.

Perhaps this is what God is seeking from us. God does not need our thanksgiving. God does not need to be soothed, appeased or persuaded. God is love and God loves us, so God seeks connection, reconnection and relationship. The act of thanksgiving can begin to open us up to the love of God, love that is always waiting for us without condition.

The 'without condition' nature of God's love revealed to us by Jesus also reshapes our understanding of the final line in today's passage. Deliverance in the day of trouble cannot be earned by sacrifice, purchased by thanksgiving or bought by anything else. Rather, God's deliverance is found in a life of connection, reconnection and relationship. Life and love are waiting. A 'thank you' may be enough to help us realise this.

Prayer

Let the phrase 'thank you' take you into prayer. Notice what comes to mind and form a prayer of thanks for each person, place or happening.
It may be as simple as 'thank you'.

IAN ADAMS

Who is wicked?

But to the wicked God says: 'What right have you to recite my stat-
utes, or take my covenant on your lips? For you hate discipline, and
you cast my words behind you. You make friends with a thief when
you see one, and you keep company with adulterers.'

So, who is wicked? The final part of Psalm 50 takes us into demanding
themes of wrongdoing, judgment and self-awareness.

Today's passage highlights how easy it is to see the wrongdoing in
others and ignore our own shortcomings. In writing 'But to the wicked
God says…', we have the clear sense that the psalmist has some other
people in mind, rather than him or herself. *They* are the wicked.

Of course, we make these kinds of judgments about other people all
the time. Jesus taught that we should not judge others (Matthew 7:1),
but it comes all too naturally to us! In our own time, whole sections of
the contemporary media (of all political persuasions) thrive on demon-
ising people not like them or us.

This does not mean we should ignore wrongdoing, but, rather, that
we need to look first to our own behaviour before pointing out the
faults of others. How might we be ignoring the life-giving promises of
God? In what ways might we be 'casting God's words behind us'?

It takes courage to be honest about ourselves—and it takes courage
to identify ourselves with those who many think of as 'wicked'. One
way that Jesus demonstrated his desire to see the best in people was to
spend time with them. He listened to strangers and conversed with
occupying soldiers. He even ate with thieves and drank with adulterers—the very behaviour denounced in this psalm…

Who, then, is wicked? The question must first be asked close to
home, with an honest appraisal of ourselves. What are we aspiring to
be? What is the direction of our lives?

Prayer

*Compassionate and demanding God, help me to face up to my own
wrongdoing and begin to make things right. Help me to avoid judging
people and to identify with those who are despised,
denounced and demonised by others.*

IAN ADAMS

Choosing words

'You give your mouth free rein for evil, and your tongue frames deceit. You sit and speak against your kin; you slander your own mother's child. These things you have done and I have been silent; you thought that I was one just like yourself. But now I rebuke you, and lay the charge before you.'

Our words are powerful things. Most of the time, of course, they simply help us to live. They enable us to find our way through the 'ordinary' happenings, actions and emotions that come up every day. They can, though, at the right moment in the right setting, bring change for good on a scale that we can barely imagine. Think of Martin Luther King's 'I have a dream…' speech.

Our words can also be immensely destructive, however. We can find ourselves carrying for the rest of our lives a single cutting remark made to us in our childhood. A relationship can be harmed seemingly beyond repair by a misplaced word or phrase and, once the words are uttered, they are out there. We cannot always delete a comment.

The psalmist's warnings about words are important. Whenever we speak without thinking, construct an untruth or bad-mouth someone close to us, we may be letting loose a destructive force into the world. The psalmist imagines the silent God, aroused by this abuse of the word, speaking a rebuke to us. We may need to hear that rebuke.

As we saw earlier this week, in the scriptures there is a great tradition of good things being spoken into being by God. It may be helpful to imagine all our words as potentially creative. Like any creative act, they may emerge best out of stillness. They will also benefit from being considered, crafted and treated with respect. At times they will also need to be provocative, inspiring and awkward, resisting everything that dehumanises.

Prayer

God the Father, call your new creation into being here. Jesus the Word, speak your life and light into being in me. Holy Spirit, whisper your joyful path into being around me and so help me to choose my words.

IAN ADAMS

Tearing apart or putting together?

'Mark this, then, you who forget God, or I will tear you apart, and there will be no one to deliver. Those who bring thanksgiving as their sacrifice honour me; to those who go the right way I will show the salvation of God.'

Are you being torn apart? Are you doing some tearing apart? Either way, it is invariably an unpleasant business, so it is tough to encounter this image, painted by the psalmist, of God being one who threatens to tear apart anyone, even those 'who forget God.' What are we to make of this?

I remember a few years ago hearing John Bell of the Iona Community suggesting in a similar situation that either God has changed or our perception of God has changed. Either way, he said, there is a cost. If *God* has changed, we have to be open to the possibility that the God who was once a tearer-apart of people could once again decide to be such. This would, in the process, paint over much of the picture of God given to us by the life of Jesus. If *our* understanding of God has changed, the cost is that even our present understanding must be a limited, provisional view on what is 'true'. I personally prefer this latter option, but either way there is a cost.

One important and helpful way to view the whole ministry of Jesus is to see it all as being about putting together what has been torn apart, remaking what is broken and restoring community. Jesus' healings can, for example, be seen primarily as ways to bring the diseased outcasts back into community. In his death on the cross, as his own body is torn apart, he is bringing together God, humanity and the whole of creation, restoring once and for all what has been broken. In these ways, Jesus 'shows the salvation of God'.

Reflection

Do you feel as if you are being torn apart? Are you doing some tearing apart? Reflect on what it might mean for you, in the way of Jesus, to be involved in putting together what has been torn apart, remaking what is broken and restoring community.

IAN ADAMS

Mercy wins

A Psalm of David, when the prophet Nathan came to him, after he had gone in to Bathsheba. Have mercy on me, O God, according to your steadfast love; according to your abundant mercy blot out my transgressions. Wash me thoroughly from my iniquity, and cleanse me from my sin.

Mercy wins. As with Psalm 50, the opening to Psalm 51 sets the tone for the rest of the psalm. This is the ground on which all that follows will rest: mercy wins. Forgiveness beats transgression. Love trumps iniquity. Whatever we have done, however low we have stooped, however ashamed we are, there is a way back. There is hope. There is restoration. There is life again.

Famously, the setting for this psalm is King David's adultery with Bathsheba and his deadly reassignment of her husband, Uriah the Hittite. David is one of the heroes of the Judeo-Christian tradition, perhaps largely because his life encompassed huge triumph and great failure. We can identify with him in both our aspirations and our weaknesses, in our achievements and our struggles. David is you and me, painted big and bold.

One of the interesting things about David's plea for mercy is that it is confident. It is not at all brash or presumptuous, but, rather, grounded in his lived experience of God's love. David knows that the character of God's mercy is abundance and God's love is steadfast. He also knows that mercy is not just passive. Mercy changes things: transgressions are blotted out, sinners are washed and cleansed.

How much at odds this is with much of the prevailing mood of our times. Whenever someone strays from the perceived correct path, our preferred options seem to be vengeance, punishment and humiliation. Thankfully, there is another way. Mercy wins.

Prayer

What is the mercy that you seek today—for yourself and for wider society? How might this psalm shape our attitudes to our own wrongdoings and the wrongdoings of others? Pray the ancient 'Jesus prayer' from the Orthodox Church: 'Lord Jesus Christ, Son of God, have mercy on me, a sinner.'

IAN ADAMS

Sinning or shining?

For I know my transgressions, and my sin is ever before me. Against you, you alone, have I sinned, and done what is evil in your sight, so that you are justified in your sentence and blameless when you pass judgment. Indeed, I was born guilty, a sinner when my mother conceived me.

How do you see yourself?

This passage from Psalm 51 takes seriously the effect that wrongdoing can have on us. It can bend us out of shape. It can taint everything. It can dominate us and, as David says in this psalm, 'my sin is ever before me'. This insight into the nature and outcome of sin is essential. Our wrongdoing is a serious matter and, if we do not face up to our sins, the consequences for ourselves and those around us can spiral out of control. Sin is a serious thing.

This psalm also highlights how our necessary acknowledgment of sin can turn into an unhealthy and damaging obsession. If our sin is all we see, we can come to imagine that our sin is what defines us. In a tragic line, the remorseful David says, 'I was born guilty.' I want to cry out, 'Please don't say that!' Far too much damage has been done by citing sinfulness as our natural state. Rather than taking sin seriously, this approach seeks to blame our sin on the way we are when we come into the world.

Much better—and much closer to the tone of the great sweep of scripture, tradition and experience—is the idea that our primal state of being carries the image of the Creator, which is characterised by beauty, love and right-doing. For 'then God said, "Let us make humankind in our image, according to our likeness"' (Genesis 1:26) and 'God saw everything that he had made, and indeed, it was very good' (v. 31).

We are not shadowy monsters who need taming, but shining creatures whose God-given and God-reflecting light needs to be restored. Begin to see yourself like this and something changes. Begin to see other people like this and everything changes!

Reflection

How do you see yourself? How do you see others? Sinning or shining?

IAN ADAMS

Desire truth

You desire truth in the inward being; therefore teach me wisdom in my secret heart. Purge me with hyssop, and I shall be clean; wash me, and I shall be whiter than snow. Let me hear joy and gladness; let the bones that you have crushed rejoice. Hide your face from my sins, and blot out all my iniquities.

Today's passage helps us to uncover a particular root of our sin problem: our disconnection. We can all too easily live our lives in compartments, in boxes, in silos. We present one face in one context and another, rather different, face in another setting. This is a process by which we gradually become disconnected within ourselves, disconnected from each other and disconnected from God, the ground of our being. We can end up barely being able to recognise ourselves.

The penitent David sees that there are disconnections between his outward actions and his inner aspirations, between his crushed bones and his dirtied skin. He senses that the antidote to this sense of disconnection is the 'desire for truth'. He has begun to live in the shadows of falsity. Now he wants to live again in the light of truth.

What might it be like to live full of truth again? To live in such a way that our actions begin to come back in tune with our inner being, ringing clear and bright? David senses that this will be a cleansing experience, one that will lead in the end to 'joy and gladness'. There really is nothing like living truthfully, living with everything connected—our aspirations and our struggles, our words and our actions—full of light and in the open.

Of course, this may be costly. Purging is not necessarily a pleasant experience, and becoming clean may require some *coming* clean. We may need to declare some things, we may need to nail some colours to masts and we may need to let go of some aspects of our lives that keep us from connection.

Prayer

Truthful God, help me to take steps into your light. Help me to begin to live in a way that is truly connected. Help me to desire truth.

IAN ADAMS

Discovering joy

Create in me a clean heart, O God, and put a new and right spirit within me. Do not cast me away from your presence, and do not take your holy spirit from me. Restore to me the joy of your salvation, and sustain in me a willing spirit.

A new year brings new opportunities. We are still close enough to the beginning of January to sense the possibility that a new year offers: a new start, a fresh beginning, another chance to be who we hope to be and to do what we hope to do.

This part of Psalm 51 has a real 'new start' feel to it. David has confessed his sins, he has submitted to a cleansing process and now he seeks a new beginning—a clean heart, a right spirit and a renewed sense of God's presence through the accompaniment of God's holy spirit. All of this will lead, senses David, to an experience of joy.

Joy cannot be bought and sold. It is deeper than happiness (as welcome as that is, of course!) and it does not depend on our circumstances. The earliest Christian communities seemed to have been characterised by joy. Life was demanding and they did not always see eye to eye, but, through it all, they seemed to have had an experience of the goodness of God that produced in them a real sense of joy.

Of course, we cannot arrange our own experience of that joy, we cannot *make* ourselves joyful, but we can participate in the process. Joy happens when, like David, we are willing to open ourselves up to, step into and immerse ourselves in God's presence. God's gift is always there, waiting for us.

Human existence has always been demanding and it remains so at this time. Perhaps one of the greatest gifts that those of us in the Judeo-Christian streams can offer to the world at this time is a life of humble joy.

Reflection

Reflect on your own experience of joy. When have you been most joyful? How would you differentiate between joy and happiness? How might you open yourself up to the possibility of God's presence today?

IAN ADAMS

Sing!

Then I will teach transgressors your ways, and sinners will return to you. Deliver me from bloodshed, O God, O God of my salvation, and my tongue will sing aloud of your deliverance.

Sing! The writer of this psalm was celebrated, among many other attributes, for his ability as a maker of music. It is natural that his love of music should surface in this psalm—'my tongue will sing aloud of your deliverance'—and the description of his singing as loud suggests that this will be exuberant. There is an important place for stillness—indeed, I spend a lot of my time teaching stillness and contemplative prayer—but there is also a vital place for exuberant thanksgiving.

The loud singing is just part of the blessing that David can sense will flow from his confession and forgiveness. This is not just about David and it is not just about us. Others may see from our experience that they, too, can take a path from wrongdoing to righteousness, from domination to freedom.

When we begin to see ourselves as we truly are—as shining creatures who need help in clearing away our accumulated debris—others may see this, too. When we address the sin that mars us without defining ourselves by our wrongdoings, others may begin to see themselves in the same light. Equally, when we step into the flow of God's presence, others may be drawn to do the same. This will be a cause for singing!

We know that David was happy to be considered strange because of his exuberant public worship: he seems to have danced with abandon when the ark of the covenant was brought back to Jerusalem (2 Samuel 6:5). There is also a long tradition in Christianity of exuberant thanksgiving. Now, there is no merit in going against the grain of who you are in this area, but however you do exuberance, perhaps today is a good day to be exuberant. You can give thanks to God in your own way for the freedoms that you have discovered in God's good care.

Reflection

Reflect on your own journey up to this point. What are you particularly thankful for? How might you give thanks today?

IAN ADAMS

Strength to be humble

O Lord, open my lips, and my mouth will declare your praise. For you have no delight in sacrifice; if I were to give a burnt offering, you would not be pleased. The sacrifice acceptable to God is a broken spirit; a broken and contrite heart, O God, you will not despise.

As we approach the end of Psalm 51, we return to a theme that we spent time with last week when we read Psalm 50—the idea of sacrifice. We saw then that the idea of literal sacrifice as helpful or even necessary has been largely discredited. God, we noted, seems to be seeking something much more interesting.

One of the challenges of reading the Psalms is that they were written in a very different society and context from our own. All-powerful lordship, obsequious servanthood and forced slavery were accepted and acceptable parts of life 3000 years ago; they are not now.

So, how might we interpret the 'sacrifice acceptable to God' in our time and in our context? How can we discover the essence of 'a broken spirit; a broken and contrite heart'? The first step may be just to recognise and accept that we do not think and talk that way now. Then, believing that the scriptures are still pregnant with divine life, we have the duty and privilege to work and pray with them to hear their message for our place, for our time.

Perhaps one way into these particular sayings is to see them as declarations of humility—not the kind of weak humility that allows itself to be walked all over, but the humility that has the strength to put our own preferences down our list of priorities in order to build connection, community and relationship with others and with God. Already today you and I may have made some simple decisions that place our interests at the centre of everything. Perhaps this part of Psalm 51 will help us to reshape our decision-making.

Prayer

Jesus, you came with all humility to be with us, alongside us, and one of us. Give me, I pray, strength to follow in your way of humility.

IAN ADAMS

Rebuild the walls!

Do good to Zion in your good pleasure; rebuild the walls of Jerusalem, then you will delight in right sacrifices, in burnt offerings and whole burnt offerings; then bulls will be offered on your altar.

Psalm 51 begins as a very personal prayer of contrition. Towards the end, it begins to ripple out in its effects. We saw on Thursday how David could imagine other people taking the same path that he had taken, from wrongdoing to righteousness, domination to freedom. At the close of the psalm, the ripples spread even further. David imagines the walls of the city of Jerusalem being rebuilt after years of neglect, shortages and warfare.

Our own journey to freedom is not just for our own benefit; the outcome is not just for us to enjoy. We are called to step into the flow of God's mission to the world (what theologians call *Missio Dei*) to play our part in God's healing of creation and look for the breaking in of what Jesus called the kingdom of God. In David's terms, it means playing our part in 'rebuilding the walls' of human society and caring for the planet.

What might this rebuilding work look like for you? Have you a sense of the walls that you are being called to rebuild? We each have our own calling. Francis of Assisi famously heard God's call to rebuild the Church. Your calling and mine will probably be smaller and more focused, but each calling is just as valued.

It is important to ask who may be rebuilding the walls with you, as rebuilding is best done in company! Do not set out on your own, if at all possible. Even more importantly, recognise that God is with you and will be taking delight in this work and in you: 'Do good to Zion in your good pleasure,' writes David (v. 18), penitent but free, fallen but restored.

Reflection

Reflect on the 'building and rebuilding' of walls that you may have already been involved in. How did you sense that was God's calling? What do you sense you might be called to build or rebuild now?

IAN ADAMS

Clothed in Christ

I have a confession: I have wanted for some years to write a series of Bible reading notes on clothes and hair in the Bible. 'Surely,' I hear you say, 'that is not a very common theme for biblical reflection?' Well, I hope you will be surprised. Both the Old and New Testaments say a fair amount about how we dress, including clothing for special occasions or roles and how we do our hair.

We all have to wear something and do something with our hair (even if it is only to shave it!) What we choose says a great deal about our commitments, our identity and how we want to be seen. My husband has a T-shirt with the slogan 'Success means never having to wear a suit', which suits him well as he is a plumber. We may wear a university tie or sweatshirt to show off our education, or a frilly, colourful skirt to convey that we are lively and creative. At my son's school, many girls wear the veil to show that they belong to a particular culture, while, as a pacifist, I was always reluctant to dress my son in the ubiquitous camouflage trousers when he was small!

Similarly, clothing and hair in both Old and New Testaments have a great deal to say about how we express our commitment to God and they can become potent symbols of what it means to be Christlike. As we explore these themes, sometimes we will encounter clothes and hair as spiritual symbols and sometimes we will receive practical advice on how it is appropriate for Christian women and men to dress and look.

Clothes and hairstyles have been and still are a matter of some controversy: should Christian women's heads be covered, as they are in some sects? Is it all right to wear jeans to church or have your ears or any other body part pierced? I am not going to answer these questions because I think that we are meant to reach our own conclusions with the aid of the Holy Spirit and our conscience. In the end, the most important decision we can make is to be 'clothed in Christ', dressed in his righteousness and love. That is an outfit we can all wear well.

Veronica Zundel

GENESIS 3:6–11, 21 (ABRIDGED)

The first cover-up

When the woman saw that the tree was good for food, and that it was a delight to the eyes, and that the tree was to be desired to make one wise, she took of its fruit and ate; and she also gave some to her husband, who was with her, and he ate. Then the eyes of both were opened, and they knew that they were naked; and they sewed fig leaves together and made loincloths for themselves... But the Lord God called to the man, and said to him, '... Who told you that you were naked? Have you eaten from the tree of which I commanded you not to eat?'... And the Lord God made garments of skins for the man and for his wife, and clothed them.

When my son was a toddler, we joked that he belonged to the NSPCC—the National Society for the Prevention of Clothing for Children! As soon as we were indoors, he seemed to want to revert to a more 'natural' state of nakedness. Animals do not need clothes...

The Bible seems to agree with my son—the fact that we need to wear clothing to 'hide' from each other is a product of our fallen state (though in the UK, especially in northern climates, it is not one we are in a hurry to reverse!) In ancient Hebrew culture, seeing another naked, except within the intimacy of marriage, brought shame on the onlooker (Genesis 9:20–25), but the attempts the primal couple make to hide (for, even in marriage, they experience shame) are woefully inadequate—we still use the term 'a fig leaf' for an unsuccessful cover-up. Instead, God provides animal skin coverings, which necessitates the first killing of animals for, before the fall, humans were only given 'every green plant' for food (1:29).

Whether you see Adam and Eve as historical or symbolic, the clothes here form a powerful image for how God provides for us, even in our fallen state of shame before him.

Reflection

Jesus said, 'And see, I am sending upon you what my Father promised; so stay here in the city until you have been clothed with power from on high' (Luke 24:49).

VERONICA ZUNDEL

Let's play dressing up

You shall make sacred vestments for the glorious adornment of your brother Aaron. And you shall speak to all who have ability, whom I have endowed with skill, that they make Aaron's vestments to consecrate him for my priesthood. These are the vestments that they shall make: a breastpiece, an ephod, a robe, a chequered tunic, a turban, and a sash. When they make these sacred vestments for your brother Aaron and his sons to serve me as priests, they shall use gold, blue, purple, and crimson yarns, and fine linen... You shall make for them linen undergarments to cover their naked flesh; they shall reach from the hips to the thighs.

When I attended an Anglican church, we had a heated debate on whether the vicar should wear vestments when leading worship or simply a clerical shirt and dog collar. The 'higher' end of the congregation wanted the full regalia and the 'lower' the simpler outfit, yet I am sure none of them would think twice about dressing in uniform for a job or 'putting on the Ritz' for a special occasion.

Wanting to wear special clothes for special roles or events is built into our humanity and, in the passage, this need is acknowledged and skilled 'designers' are called on to fulfil it. It is just the beginning of a long description of the priestly garments: the ephod adorned with stones engraved with the names of the twelve tribes and the breastplate with twelve different jewels—it's worth reading the whole chapter just for the glorious words. Even the underwear was specified—so that worshippers should not be embarrassed if the robe blew up in the wind, perhaps! All this was to convey to the people the glory and holiness of the God whose worship the priests were conducting.

Under our 'high priest', Jesus (Hebrews 4:14), we are all priests (1 Peter 2:4–5). Whether we wear white robes to church, like many Africans, or turn up in jeans, we are still 'a living sacrifice, holy and acceptable to God' (Romans 12:1). So, let's not judge each other by what we wear.

Prayer

Lord, with you every day is special. Let me be dressed every day in your holiness.

Veronica Zundel

A mother's offering

Samuel was ministering before the Lord, a boy wearing a linen ephod. His mother used to make for him a little robe and take it to him each year, when she went up with her husband to offer the yearly sacrifice. Then Eli would bless Elkanah and his wife, and say, 'May the Lord repay you with children by this woman for the gift that she made to the Lord'... And the Lord took note of Hannah; she conceived and bore three sons and two daughters. And the boy Samuel grew up in the presence of the Lord.

In my teenage years, my mother—who was not a great seamstress—made some complicated clothes for me. I especially remember a brown mini-dress with a beige pintucked inset and covered buttons with fabric loops. I guess her efforts showed how much she loved me.

I find today's little story deeply touching. Like Hannah, I have suffered infertility and then had a 'miracle' son. Just imagine this woman, who has willingly separated herself from her precious firstborn, going to see him once a year, each year with a slightly bigger priestly robe (she must have had to guess how much bigger to make it). Making clothes for him was the only regular act of love she could offer him—though I am sure she would have prayed for him constantly.

In a sense, all parenting is a process of letting go, as we lose a baby to gain a toddler, lose a toddler to gain a schoolchild, lose a child to gain a teenager and, eventually, if all goes well, our children leave home and set up their own lives and families. Yet, our love for our changing offspring does not diminish as they change; it just has to be expressed differently.

Does God, too, express love for us in different ways as we grow in our Christian life? The 'garments'—certain styles of worship or ethical opinions—that we wear as Christians may come to feel too tight, but I believe God provides us with new ways of acknowledging and serving him—new outfits, as it were.

Reflection

Change is not necessarily decay—it may be growth.

Veronica Zundel

38

2 Samuel 13:15–19 (abridged)

Garments of sorrow

Then Amnon was seized with a very great loathing for her; indeed, his loathing was even greater than the lust he had felt for her. Amnon said to her, 'Get out!' But she said to him, 'No, my brother; for this wrong in sending me away is greater than the other that you did to me.' But he... called the young man who served him and said, 'Put this woman out of my presence, and bolt the door after her.' (Now she was wearing a long robe with sleeves; for this is how the virgin daughters of the king were clothed in earlier times.) So his servant put her out, and bolted the door after her. But Tamar put ashes on her head, and tore the long robe that she was wearing; she put her hand on her head, and went away, crying aloud as she went.

It is shocking to reflect that among your female friends there is almost certainly at least one who has been raped. Most victims are raped by someone they know, some by a relative when they are only children.

Tamar was raped by her half-brother while she was bringing him food. His reaction afterwards gives support to the suggestion that rape is not an act of desire but of hatred. Jewish law said that Amnon should compensate by marrying her—no one else would want to marry a 'defiled' woman and singleness meant economic destitution. Instead, with extreme cruelty, he banishes her.

So, it is not surprising that Tamar tears her clothes in the time-honoured manner of Jewish mourners. Orthodox Jews still make a little tear in their lapel when a relative has died. A 'long robe with sleeves' was a luxury garment (remember the one made by Jacob for his favourite son Joseph: Genesis 37:3). Now it becomes an outward expression of Tamar's inward pain. Her special clothes are no longer a sign of festivity but of tragedy.

Reflection

What are you sad or angry about today? How can you best express this to God?

Veronica Zundel

Try this for size

When David had finished speaking to Saul, the soul of Jonathan was bound to the soul of David, and Jonathan loved him as his own soul... Then Jonathan made a covenant with David, because he loved him as his own soul. Jonathan stripped himself of the robe that he was wearing, and gave it to David, and his armour, and even his sword and his bow and his belt. David went out and was successful wherever Saul sent him; as a result, Saul set him over the army. And all the people, even the servants of Saul, approved.

It must have been around 1968, and my schoolfriend and I had gone out and bought trendy mini-dresses for the princely sum of £2.50 each. When we arrived at the church youth club wearing them, we ran to the Ladies and exchanged dresses. Of course, we had to change back quickly into our normal clothes when my dad came to collect us! I suppose we were trying out how it would feel to be someone else (as a little girl does when she totters around in her mum's stilettos).

Swapping, giving or lending clothes can be a sign of friendship, as it was for David and Jonathan. When a boy puts his coat round a girl's shoulders on a cold day, she knows their relationship is progressing! I am particularly struck by Jonathan giving David his armour, as, earlier in his life, when he faced Goliath, David had rejected Saul's armour as too big for him (1 Samuel 17:38–39). Now, David is fully grown and his friend Jonathan's armour fits fine. Perhaps there is a deliberate contrast here, for David's relationship with Saul was never easy, but with Saul's son, Jonathan, there is never any conflict.

Our sense of identity comes not only from what we do or how we dress but also from our relationships with others. Sometimes we want to be defined in our own right, not just as our children's dad or mum or our boss's employee. Still, our main sense of who we are comes from how others relate to us. Above all, our primary identity is found in Jesus, as a child of God (Luke 6:35–36).

Prayer

Jesus, dress me in yourself.

Veronica Zundel

Hair-raising

You shall not round off the hair on your temples or mar the edges of your beard... There was a certain man of Zorah, of the tribe of the Danites, whose name was Manoah. His wife was barren, having borne no children. And the angel of the Lord appeared to the woman and said to her, 'Although you are barren, having borne no children, you shall conceive and bear a son. Now be careful not to drink wine or strong drink, or to eat anything unclean, for you shall conceive and bear a son. No razor is to come on his head, for the boy shall be a nazirite to God from birth. It is he who shall begin to deliver Israel from the hand of the Philistines.'

Near where I live in north London, you can often see Orthodox Jewish men and boys with their side curls peeping out from their hats or skull-caps. They take literally the command not to cut the sides of their hair. I also know an Australian Christian activist who wears his hair (though he is white) in long dreadlocks. When he was imprisoned for a protest in the UK, he claimed religious exemption from having his head shaved, saying he had taken a Nazirite vow (this was a special vow of commitment to God, taken by Samson's mother on his behalf, and perhaps also by John the Baptist).

Our appearance can still show our core values today. 'Plain people', such as the Amish, show their loyalty to God by their modest clothing, covered hair for women and the same simple haircut for all men. Other Christians dress like everyone else.

Christians have disagreed vociferously over issues such as short hair or trousers for women or head coverings, but surely the important thing is that we honour God in everything we do, including our clothes and hair. We are not called to be dowdy, but we are to dress in a way that does not tempt, distract or offend—for instance, wearing black for a funeral or dressing simply when preaching or leading worship.

Reflection

'For the kingdom of God is not food and drink [or clothes and hair!] but righteousness and peace and joy in the Holy Spirit' (Romans 14:17).

VERONICA ZUNDEL

Pride before a fall

Now in all Israel there was no one to be praised so much for his beauty as Absalom... When he cut the hair of his head... he weighed the hair of his head, two hundred shekels by the king's weight... Absalom was riding on his mule, and the mule went under the thick branches of a great oak. His head caught fast in the oak, and he was left hanging between heaven and earth, while the mule that was under him went on... And ten young men, Joab's armour-bearers, surrounded Absalom and struck him, and killed him... The king was deeply moved, and went up to the chamber over the gate, and wept; and as he went, he said, 'O my son Absalom, my son, my son Absalom! Would I had died instead of you, O Absalom, my son, my son!'

David had several sons and it was by no means clear which of them would succeed him, so Absalom starts a succession war, but, like the prodigal son, he wants the kingship before David is even dead (2 Samuel 15:10). What Absalom has forgotten—or perhaps never heard—is the story of Samuel's choice of David as successor to Saul. David is young and insignificant, but, when Samuel looks for a king among Jesse's sons, God rejects every one, except David: 'for the Lord does not see as mortals see; they look on the outward appearance, but the Lord looks on the heart' (1 Samuel 16:7).

Is Absalom, for all his glamour, really a good candidate for king? He took vicious vengeance on his half-brother Amnon for the rape of Tamar, burned commander Joab's field and even slept with his father's concubines. Yet, David, like God, still loves Absalom enough to die for him. This fact suggests to me that David is Jesus' ancestor spiritually as well as genetically.

We may think we are too sophisticated to judge by appearances, but, ever since US presidential candidates have appeared on television, the electorate have never chosen the shorter of two candidates. The exterior is not necessarily a measure of a person's character!

Reflection
Good things may come in plain packages.

VERONICA ZUNDEL

Letting her hair down

A woman in the city, who was a sinner, having learned that [Jesus] was eating in the Pharisee's house, brought an alabaster jar of ointment. She stood behind him at his feet, weeping, and began to bathe his feet with her tears and to dry them with her hair. Then she continued kissing his feet and anointing them with the ointment. Now when the Pharisee who had invited him saw it, he said to himself, 'If this man were a prophet, he would have known who and what kind of woman this is who is touching him—that she is a sinner.'

Even if the Pharisee had not known who the woman was, it would have been clear from her actions that she was a woman 'of ill repute'. First of all, she uncovered her hair in mixed company, which no respectable woman would ever do. Second, she then brazenly used it as a towel to dry Jesus' feet and, perhaps worst of all, she proceeded to kiss his feet repeatedly—an action that would surely raise eyebrows even in our more liberal society.

That Jesus lets all this happen is, in the Pharisee's eyes, a clear indication that he has no spiritual wisdom. In fact, Jesus has a greater, and deeper, wisdom than just adherence to the social rules. His yardstick is that of love rather than respectability. So, he tells a story of two debtors—one owing much and the other owing little—whose debts are both cancelled and asks, 'Which of them will love [the creditor] more?' The Pharisee knows the right answer—'The one for whom he cancelled the greater debt'—but he's not off the hook yet. Jesus goes on to rebuke him for his lack of hospitality, in that he has neither had Jesus' feet washed nor anointed them, as would have been proper in those days (vv. 40–46). Clearly the host has little love for this wayward prophet.

Reflection

Sometimes God may call us to an action that seems like madness. It may involve us looking foolish, even sinful. Yet, if we are brave enough to take the risk, we may find unexpected blessing.

VERONICA ZUNDEL

God the tailor

[Jesus said] 'Therefore I tell you, do not worry about your life, what you will eat or what you will drink, or about your body, what you will wear. Is not life more than food, and the body more than clothing? Look at the birds of the air; they neither sow nor reap nor gather into barns, and yet your heavenly Father feeds them. Are you not of more value than they? And can any of you by worrying add a single hour to your span of life? And why do you worry about clothing? Consider the lilies of the field, how they grow; they neither toil nor spin, yet I tell you, even Solomon in all his glory was not clothed like one of these.'

I'm sure I'm not the only one who stands before a full wardrobe and says, 'I have nothing to wear'! We are used to having more clothes than we can stuff into our drawers, but, for the people Jesus was speaking to, the poor and dispossessed, their worries were probably more about if they could afford enough cloth to cover them decently. Workers wore short robes not only for reasons of practicality but also because a long robe was a luxury item. Millions of people in today's world are in a similar position, wearing rags or other people's cast-offs. How poignant must God's promise in Revelation 3:5 seem to them: 'If you conquer, you will be clothed… in white robes'. In the affluent West, most (though by no means all) of us do not need to worry too much about clothes—or food.

For some of us, this is the hardest of Jesus' commandments to follow—those who are inclined to worry will do so regardless. Jesus, ever a lover of nature, points us to how God provides for the natural world. A poem by D.H. Lawrence observes that he has never seen 'a wild thing' feeling sorry for itself. Should we be more confident that God will provide what we truly need—whether it is food, clothes, hugs, a partner or a family? There are no guarantees, but worrying is certainly not a way to provide for oneself.

Prayer

Lord, make me a spiritual warrior, not an unspiritual worrier.

VERONICA ZUNDEL

Dressed for work

During supper Jesus, knowing that the Father had given all things into his hands, and that he had come from God and was going to God, got up from the table, took off his outer robe, and tied a towel around himself. Then he poured water into a basin and began to wash the disciples' feet and to wipe them with the towel that was tied around him.

When I had to wear school uniform, the school's justification was that it would remove signs of different social status between the pupils, but, in reality, it was easy to tell which students' families were poorer as they had cheaper versions of the uniform or fewer spare items, which meant that their clothes were always dirty. From a duchess to a down-and-out, clothes show our social standing like nothing else.

Here Jesus puts on the humble garb of a servant. We know he had a high-class seamless robe (John 19:23), which some have identified as a festive garment, probably worn for this Passover meal. Jesus now puts a towel around his waist, so that he can kneel to wash his friends' feet— a servant's job (perhaps there were no servants there, to keep the meeting secret). As Philippians 2:7 describes, he 'emptied himself, taking the form of a slave'.

In Coventry Cathedral, there is a Chapel of Christ the Servant with the words 'I am among you as one who serves' (Luke 22:27) set into the floor in metal letters. Except when we sing 'The Servant King', this aspect of Jesus does not seem to be emphasised often in churches today. Perhaps it is time we rediscovered it.

If we have an understanding of Jesus as a servant to humanity, then, as we follow him, we will also understand our own mission as one of service, as we imitate him. We may need practical outer clothes for the service God calls us to—an apron, perhaps, or dungarees—but what 'spiritual clothes', what virtues and spiritual gifts, might we also need for a life of service?

Reflection

Who has God called me to serve today? It may not be in some glamorous ministry—it may be just to serve your partner and family.

VERONICA ZUNDEL

45

As at the beginning

When the soldiers had crucified Jesus, they took his clothes and divided them into four parts, one for each soldier. They also took his tunic; now the tunic was seamless, woven in one piece from the top. So they said to one another, 'Let us not tear it, but cast lots for it to see who will get it.' This was to fulfil what the scripture says, 'They divided my clothes among themselves, and for my clothing they cast lots.' And that is what the soldiers did.

Many scholars agree that Jesus was probably completely naked on the cross—but few artists have had the courage to portray him that way! To be stripped naked by others—or to be ordered to take off all our clothes—is to lose dignity and self-respect. Jesus on the cross thus becomes the essence of vulnerable, defenceless humanity, not even protected by clothing.

Perhaps there is another dimension here, too. Paul speaks of Christ as the second Adam (1 Corinthians 15:45–48). The first Adam, the archetypal human being, was naked and unashamed before the fall; the last Adam is naked, too, as he identifies with fallen humanity and restores us to wholeness and innocence. Jesus has taken all our weakness and vulnerability on himself.

A little side note: as mentioned yesterday, a tunic woven in one piece was a valuable piece of clothing that Jesus, as an itinerant preacher, could certainly not have afforded. Someone loved him very much to give him such a special garment. Maybe it was one of the well-off women who followed him (Luke 8:1–3). Yet, this precious gift went to hardened soldiers.

At the transfiguration, we are told, Jesus' clothes glowed brilliant white, whiter than any bleach could make them (Mark 9:2–3). Here, on the cross, he has, in Isaiah's words, 'no form or majesty that we should look at him, nothing in his appearance that we should desire him' (Isaiah 53:2). If we ever feel 'stripped bare', emotionally or physically, we can know Jesus has been there with us, in the darkest place.

Reflection

'I was naked and you gave me clothing' (Matthew 25:36).

VERONICA ZUNDEL

How to be well dressed

I desire, then, that in every place the men should pray, lifting up holy hands without anger or argument; also that the women should dress themselves modestly and decently in suitable clothing, not with their hair braided, or with gold, pearls, or expensive clothes, but with good works, as is proper for women who profess reverence for God.

What is 'suitable clothing' for women? What does it mean to dress 'modestly and decently'? I fear that the answers to this question have usually been decided by men—possibly by men who want to hide 'their' women from other men. It is true, though, that in countries where women are veiled, some women say they feel liberated by the veil from men's appraising stares. (Incidentally, these injunctions apply to men, too—provocatively dressed men, for instance with their shirts off, can be just as much of a temptation to women!)

We do not have to read these prescriptions about clothing as a restriction on women. They could be saying, 'Women: don't think your only value is in your appearance. God is more interested in your character, and men should be, too.' In other words, our best adornment is the good things we do for others, not gold and pearls (materials of which, I must admit, I am quite fond!) Women are created, like men, to do 'good works'. This also means that ageing and loss of youthful beauty does not take away their worth.

Peter agrees with the writer of Timothy: 'Do not adorn yourselves outwardly by braiding your hair, and by wearing gold ornaments or fine clothing; rather, let your adornment be the inner self with the lasting beauty of a gentle and quiet spirit, which is very precious in God's sight' (1 Peter 3:3–4). Having a 'gentle and quiet spirit' does not mean women should be like mice and never speak out. If you are in any doubt about that, read Mary's prophetic and political Magnificat again (Luke 1:46–56). Ultimately, a gentle inner self and outward works of caring are things that we should all display, both women and men.

Prayer

Lord, help me to know what 'modest and decent' dress means in my culture.

Veronica Zundel

Get your clothes on

As God's chosen ones, holy and beloved, clothe yourselves with compassion, kindness, humility, meekness, and patience. Bear with one another and, if anyone has a complaint against another, forgive each other; just as the Lord has forgiven you, so you also must forgive. Above all, clothe yourselves with love, which binds everything together in perfect harmony. And let the peace of Christ rule in your hearts, to which indeed you were called in the one body. And be thankful.

Are you ever tempted to enter one of those competitions where the prize is a large amount of money to spend on clothes? If you won, you could at last have that made-to-measure suit or cashmere coat… Being dressed well can give confidence, a sense of status and power, although there are always those who feel much happier in old jeans and a sloppy jumper! Indeed, all of us prefer the clothes we feel most comfortable in.

Today's passage tells us that God has prepared a set of perfectly fitting clothes for us—no need to win a competition. Compassion, kindness, humility, meekness and patience are already available to us, for they are the qualities of Jesus, who longs to clothe us in them. When we first try to put them on, they may feel too big—like Saul's armour for David or someone else's clothes—but, as we put them on every day, gradually they will come to feel as natural as our own skin, the most comfortable outfit we have ever worn. It may take years, but if we practise wearing them, we will make them our own.

I phoned my mother on a freezing night not so long ago and she reminded me to wrap up warm (I don't know why she still thinks I need telling, at nearly 60!) Paul, writing to the Colossians, reminds us to wrap up in the warmest garment there is—love. If we do not have love, we will be forever shivering in the cold of conflict and loneliness.

God does not force these clothes on us; we have to make a conscious choice to wear them: 'clothe yourselves'.

Prayer
Lord, teach me to clothe myself with gratitude.

VERONICA ZUNDEL

Clothes that do not wear out

For we know that if the earthly tent we live in is destroyed, we have a building from God, a house not made with hands, eternal in the heavens. For in this tent we groan, longing to be clothed with our heavenly dwelling—if indeed, when we have taken it off we will not be found naked. For while we are still in this tent, we groan under our burden, because we wish not to be unclothed but to be further clothed, so that what is mortal may be swallowed up by life. He who has prepared us for this very thing is God.

The older I get and the more fascinating science programmes I watch, the more I love this beautiful, complex world God has brought into being. Scientists tell us that if conditions on earth were even slightly different, then life, and we ourselves, could not have emerged here. It really does seem that God wanted us to exist!

Yes, I know 1 John 2:15 tells us, 'Do not love the world or the things in the world', but I do not think he means us to hate God's creation. Rather, we are not to be ruled by 'the desire of the flesh, the desire of the eyes, the pride in riches' (v. 16)—greed, which wants to own things and people rather than just to rejoice in them.

It is a natural human feeling to be attached to 'this tent', as Paul refers to the human body and the physical world. It is also natural to be frustrated with its limitations, especially as we age. Paul recognises that we do not want to become nothing, to lose our individuality (which is often expressed in our clothes). So he reassures us that the 'new heavens and new earth' will not be like being stripped bare—rather, it will be everything that is good in this mortal world, being absorbed into a far greater, eternal world. God is not intending to waste this wonderful world in which he has 'clothed' us, but to transform it into something even more wonderful.

Reflection

'If there is a physical body, there is also a spiritual body'
(1 Corinthians 15:44).

Veronica Zundel

Jesus' wisdom in Luke

These readings cover extracts from four key chapters of Luke's Gospel, concentrating not on the accounts of miracles or the parables but Jesus' teaching—his 'wisdom'. Wisdom was to be one of the marks of the Messiah: the promised descendant of David was going to be filled with the 'spirit of wisdom' (Isaiah 11:2). This wisdom is a God-given attribute. It is more than intelligence or knowledge—insight, vision and understanding are its roots. According to Proverbs 3:19, it was 'by wisdom' that the creation took place, and the description of Jesus as 'the Word' (John 1:1) picks up the same idea. Indeed, *logos* in Greek (the root of our word 'logic') speaks of revealed meaning. 'Without [the Word] not one thing came into being' (John 1:3). We live in a universe that makes sense!

As we look at Jesus' wisdom, we shall see that it goes far beyond clever or sensible arguments. This is divine wisdom, a revelation of the mind of God. Not surprisingly, it sometimes seems to contradict conventional human logic. The poor are happy and the despised are blessed, while the rich, powerful and famous are in danger of judgment. Enemies are to be loved, offenders forgiven, loans made without expectation of return. In human terms, it is crazy, but this is the lifestyle of the kingdom of heaven.

Not only that, but here was a man—the 'Son of Man' as he called himself, the unique 'divine/human' who was sent by God (Daniel 7:13, 14)—recruiting followers on the basis that they should deny themselves, take up their cross, and follow him (Mark 8:34). His destiny, he assured them, was execution on one of those crosses. In the circumstances, it is a marvel that he recruited anybody, yet there were the Twelve (named in these chapters) and the 120 (Acts 1:15) and others, too, who saw in this teacher something extraordinary and in his teaching something sublime. They followed him to Golgotha, then to the empty tomb and the upper room at Pentecost. I suspect that they did so because they had never heard teaching like this, but then the world had never had a teacher like this either.

David Winter

Generous gift or tiresome burden?

[Jesus] said to [the Pharisees], 'The Son of Man is lord of the sabbath'... He entered the synagogue and taught, and there was a man there whose right hand was withered. The scribes and the Pharisees watched him to see whether he would cure on the sabbath, so that they might find an accusation against him. Even though he knew what they were thinking, he said to the man who had the withered hand, 'Come and stand here.' He got up and stood there. Then Jesus said to them, 'I ask you, is it lawful to do good or to do harm on the sabbath, to save life or to destroy it?' After looking around at all of them, he said to him, 'Stretch out your hand.' He did so, and his hand was restored.

Long ago, humans discovered that they would be healthier and happier if they allowed themselves a regular break from work. Accordingly, most cultures recognised a regular 'day of rest'. For the Jews, this became a divinely ordained institution—the weekly sabbath, seen as celebrating God's 'rest' after he completed the 'work' of creation. It was to be a 'sabbath to the Lord your God' (Exodus 20:10), to be observed on the seventh day of the week, Saturday. Individuals were forbidden to do any kind of work and, equally, they were not to make others work—slaves, people of other nationalities, even their animals.

By the time of Jesus, the sabbath was strictly enforced, with a whole library of detailed rules. There is quite a lot about Jesus and the sabbath in the Gospels—stories like the one above, and his teaching about its true meaning. It would be wrong to assume that Jesus was against the whole idea. In fact, here he was expressing his frustration that a generous gift of God was being distorted into a tiresome burden. The 'Son of Man' is 'lord of the sabbath' (Luke 6:5). The divine healer will do his gracious work whatever day of the week it is!

Reflection

Sunday, the Christian sabbath, is an opportunity to enjoy God's 'generous gift' without making it a 'tiresome burden'.

DAVID WINTER

Good news—and bad news

Then [Jesus] looked up at his disciples and said: 'Blessed are you who are poor, for yours is the kingdom of God. Blessed are you who are hungry now, for you will be filled. Blessed are you who weep now, for you will laugh. Blessed are you when people hate you, and when they exclude you, revile you, and defame you on account of the Son of Man. Rejoice in that day and leap for joy, for surely your reward is great in heaven; for that is what their ancestors did to the prophets. But woe to you who are rich, for you have received your consolation. Woe to you who are full now, for you will be hungry. Woe to you who are laughing now, for you will mourn and weep. Woe to you when all speak well of you, for that is what their ancestors did to the false prophets.'

Here is a perfect example of the 'upside-down' teaching of the kingdom of God. The poor are blessed; the rich are cursed. The hungry are fed; the full are hungry. Those who weep are happy; those who laugh are sad. The so-called 'Beatitudes' (Matthew 5:1–12) have an almost identical message and so does the song of Mary, the 'Magnificat' (Luke 1:46–55): the mighty are cast down and the humble and meek are exalted. Luke's version in our passage today is blunter. In Matthew, it is the 'poor in heart' who inherit the kingdom of heaven, but here it is simply 'the poor'. There is, he implies, a blessing that is peculiar to the powerless. Those who are utterly dependent know what it is to trust God.

Of course, this teaching must be read against the background of the whole story of Jesus. He did not hate the rich: his ministry was funded by wealthy women disciples (8:3), and he was buried in the tomb of a wealthy supporter (23:50–53). His good news was for all, but, to be blessed by it, both rich and poor must repent and believe, and that would, it seems, be easier for the poor than the rich (18:24).

Reflection

O may no earth-born cloud arise
to hide Thee from Thy servant's eyes.

John Keble (1827)

DAVID WINTER

The golden rule

'But I say to you that listen, love your enemies, do good to those who hate you, bless those who curse you, pray for those who abuse you. If anyone strikes you on the cheek, offer the other also; and from anyone who takes away your coat do not withhold even your shirt. Give to everyone who begs from you; and if anyone takes away your goods, do not ask for them again. Do to others as you would have them do to you.'

As I sat down to reflect on this Bible passage, the radio was reporting a series of attacks on Christian churches in Nigeria. Worshippers had been killed and their places of worship destroyed by bombs. They knew who was responsible—militant Islamists. What should their response be? Revenge? Teaching the enemy some kind of lesson? Simply working to improve security, trusting the police and saying their prayers?

On the basis of this passage, the answer is clear, if extremely challenging. They should 'turn the other cheek', show love to their enemies, bless and pray for them. They should overcome evil with good. That, says Jesus, is the kingdom way. Welcome to the revolutionary world of the Messiah!

Of course, Jesus was not setting out a manifesto for government. If so, Christians should have 'turned the other cheek' to Hitler's advancing army and allowed our Jewish fellow citizens to be carted off to concentration camps. In many ways, that is a relatively easy one, of course, but what about 'peace-keeping' that ends up involving violence, or wars waged to defend national interests or prosperity? Jesus was speaking to the citizens of the new kingdom and, in a deliberately exaggerated way, setting out the most difficult choices they would face in following his path of self-giving love. That is not how to police an unredeemed society, but it *is* how Christ's new people could show the world a model of what the kingdom of heaven is like.

Reflection

There is a 'golden rule' in this passage that is true for both the disciple and everyone else: 'Do to others as you would have them do to you'
(Luke 6:31).

David Winter

Standing in judgment

'Do not judge, and you will not be judged; do not condemn, and
you will not be condemned. Forgive, and you will be forgiven; give,
and it will be given to you. A good measure, pressed down, shaken
together, running over, will be put into your lap; for the measure
you give will be the measure you get back... Why do you see the
speck in your neighbour's eye, but do not notice the log in your
own eye? Or how can you say to your neighbour, "Friend, let me
take out the speck in your eye", when you yourself do not see the
log in your own eye? You hypocrite, first take the log out of your
own eye, and then you will see clearly to take the speck out of
your neighbour's eye.'

A great theme that runs throughout the Bible is that there is only one
true judge—God. In his teaching here, Jesus warns his disciples against
trying to usurp that unique role themselves. It is not our responsibility
to pass judgments on others (although it is a very popular human exer-
cise!) On the other hand, those who are generous in their judgments of
others will find that our heavenly judge is also generous to them. Those
who forgive are themselves forgiven. Those who give generously are
generously blessed. That is the logic of grace: we do not 'earn' blessing
by 'being good', but the gracious heart is open to grace.

Jesus, then, offers a ludicrous picture of a person who has got a
whole log in his eye offering to remove a tiny speck from his neighbour's eye. Of course, he can't do it as the wretched log keeps getting
in the way and he can't see what he is doing. Jesus, no doubt, gets a
laugh, but then the crowd sees what he is getting at. The lesson is that
only those who recognise their own faults can 'see clearly' to help others—or receive God's forgiveness themselves.

Reflection
*We should repent of our own sins before we dare to judge the sins of others.
Not a bad thought for Ash Wednesday!*

DAVID WINTER

Walking the talk

'Why do you call me "Lord, Lord" and do not do what I tell you? I will show you what someone is like who comes to me, hears my words, and acts on them. That one is like a man building a house, who dug deeply and laid the foundation on rock; when a flood arose, the river burst against that house but could not shake it, because it had been well built. But the one who hears and does not act is like a man who built a house on the ground without a foundation. When the river burst against it, immediately it fell, and great was the ruin of that house.'

One of the major (if rather obscure) debates in church history has been the relationship between 'faith' and 'works', the question of whether we are saved by what we believe or by what we do. To the preacher Jesus, I think this would have been what we call today a no-brainer—a question with an obvious answer. If you truly believe that Jesus is the Messiah and Son of God, then why would you not do what he says? If you do not do what he commands, then you cannot really believe in him. It is as simple as that!

The story that Jesus tells of the wise and foolish builders drives the message home. The one who hears the teaching of Jesus and lives by it, 'acts' on it, is like somebody who is building on a sound foundation. By contrast, the one who hears but does nothing about it is heading for ruin. In this sense, at least, faith and works are the same thing. What we believe inevitably shapes what we do.

It all hinges on our understanding of the word 'faith'. In this context, it does not mean 'the faith'—the creed, propositions about the nature of God or the meaning of eternal life—but is essentially trust. Do you believe and trust in Jesus? If we trust him, we shall set out (however unworthily) to do what he commands.

Reflection

*Jesus said, 'If you love me, you will keep my commandments' (John 14:15).
Of course you will!*

DAVID WINTER

Never satisfied!

'To what then will I compare the people of this generation, and what are they like? They are like children sitting in the marketplace and calling to one another, "We played the flute for you, and you did not dance; we wailed, and you did not weep." For John the Baptist has come eating no bread and drinking no wine, and you say, "He has a demon"; the Son of Man has come eating and drinking, and you say, "Look, a glutton and a drunkard, a friend of tax collectors and sinners!" Nevertheless, wisdom is vindicated by all her children.'

Earlier in this chapter (vv. 20–23), we are told of John the Baptist, now imprisoned, sending some of his disciples to ask Jesus if he is truly the 'one who is to come' foretold by the prophets. Jesus sent the disciples back to John with a simple message: tell the people what you have seen and heard—miracles, healings, and good news for the poor. This would have answered John's doubts. Today's passage follows on from this episode and deals with the issue of having the wisdom to recognise God's purpose.

Why had the crowds gone out to the wilderness to hear John preach? They had seen and heard a prophet, said Jesus, 'and more than a prophet' (v. 26)—the messenger who would precede the coming of the Messiah, no less. Yet still the crowds were unsure. John was strange. He lived an austere life, feeding on 'locusts and wild honey', dressed in animal skins (Mark 1:6). They were not sure about Jesus, either. He was the exact opposite. He ate and drank (even at the tables of 'sinners'). Their reactions reminded Jesus of a song the children sang, about those who would neither dance for the flautists nor weep with the wailers.

As so often, Jesus makes his point in one telling final sentence. They needed to recognise the wisdom of God's purpose, which could work through both the austerity of John and the warmth of Jesus. Wisdom's children, the people of the kingdom, would find no contradiction in that.

Reflection

Recognising the work of God, even in unlikely ways, is wisdom's gift.

DAVID WINTER

Forgiveness works; love wins

'A certain creditor had two debtors; one owed five hundred denarii, and the other fifty. When they could not pay, he cancelled the debts for both of them. Now which of them will love him more?' Simon [the Pharisee] answered, 'I suppose the one for whom he cancelled the greater debt.' And Jesus said to him, 'You have judged rightly.' Then turning towards the woman, he said to Simon, 'Do you see this woman? I entered your house; you gave me no water for my feet, but she has bathed my feet with her tears and dried them with her hair. You gave me no kiss, but from the time I came in she has not stopped kissing my feet. You did not anoint my head with oil, but she has anointed my feet with ointment. Therefore, I tell you, her sins, which were many, have been forgiven; hence she has shown great love. But the one to whom little is forgiven, loves little.'

Here are two stories that share one message. One is a kind of parable, telling of two debtors who are forgiven their debts, one for a sum ten times greater than the other. Which debtor is the more grateful? The answer is easy: the one who owed more.

The second story is actually happening then and there, at the dinner party at the house of Simon the Pharisee, much to the host's embarrassment. A woman 'who was a sinner' (v. 37) had slipped into the party and was washing Jesus' feet with her tears, drying them with her long hair (a sign of her 'trade') and anointing them with oil. Luke, the master storyteller, adds many wonderful details, including the words of Jesus to Simon, 'Do you see this woman?' Of course he did, but we can be pretty sure that he was trying not to! Jesus pointed out that she had offered him all the courtesies due to an honoured guest (which Simon had omitted to do). What was her motivation? The same as the forgiven debtor. She had been forgiven much and therefore loved much.

Reflection

Here is the good news of Jesus in one vivid scene:
forgiveness works; love wins.

DAVID WINTER

Sowing and reaping

When a great crowd gathered and people from town after town came to [Jesus], he said in a parable: 'A sower went out to sow his seed; and as he sowed, some fell on the path and was trampled on, and the birds of the air ate it up. Some fell on the rock; and as it grew up, it withered for lack of moisture. Some fell among thorns, and the thorns grew with it and choked it. Some fell into good soil, and when it grew, it produced a hundredfold.' As he said this, he called out, 'Let anyone with ears to hear listen!'

Is this a story about the sower, or is it about the seed or the soil? So far as we are told, there is nothing wrong with the farmer's technique here—the seed is scattered widely over the ground. Neither is there anything wrong with the seed, which represents the message of the kingdom of God. The soil is a different matter, because some of it is hard, some full of weeds, some stony—and some is good and fertile. The soil cannot do anything about itself, though, can it?

The usual interpretation of this well-known parable concentrates on the soil. It warns against the hard heart, the stony soul and the life so caught up in the 'weeds' of the world that the saving message fails to thrive. In that case, the parable is directed at the hearers of the message. The good news will take root in the open, longing heart, unencumbered by worldly distractions, which is the interpretation offered in the following verses (vv. 11–15).

Jesus, however, generally followed the practice of the rabbis—he told a story and left his hearers to ponder its meaning ('Let anyone with ears to hear listen', v. 8). Rather than seeing this as a warning of failure (only one seed in four germinates), the disciples could equally well hear it as a source of encouragement. After all, it ends with a massive harvest ('a hundredfold'). They should take heart!

Reflection

However unpromising the soil (and, indeed, however inept the sower),
the seed of the gospel will produce a great harvest.

DAVID WINTER

Let your light shine

'No one after lighting a lamp hides it under a jar, or puts it under a bed, but puts it on a lampstand, so that those who enter may see the light. For nothing is hidden that will not be disclosed, nor is anything secret that will not become known and come to light. Then pay attention to how you listen; for to those who have, more will be given; and from those who do not have, even what they seem to have will be taken away.'

There are three gems of wisdom here from Jesus the teacher, all connected with 'light'. The first is a call to his disciples not to hide the light of their allegiance to him under a jar or beneath the bed. Many of us do this, sometimes out of modesty, sometimes out of embarrassment, sometimes because we do not want to be publicly labelled as 'religious'. 'Let your light shine', says Jesus (Matthew 5:16). 'Shine like stars in the world', says Paul (Philippians 2:15). Jesus is the 'light of the world' (John 8:12), but we are reflectors of his light. If we hide that light, the world is darker.

The second message is about disclosure. In the end, everything will be revealed: there will be no secrets. It is, in any case, futile to try to hide the truth about our failures from ourselves (because memory and conscience will do their work), from others (because things tend to come out: Numbers 32:23), or, most of all, from God, who knows all about us (Psalm 139:1).

The third follows from that. Listen! Hear the message of the kingdom: repentance, faith, forgiveness. Those who are open to its light will have 'more and more', the abundant life of the kingdom. Those who close their ears or shut their eyes will lose even their cherished heritage as children of the covenant.

Reflection

At first sight, these are solemn words—a warning, indeed. Yet, they are also a promise. The light has come into the world with Jesus and the darkness cannot overcome it (John 1:5). To be open to that light is to be brought 'out of darkness into his marvellous light' (1 Peter 2:9).

DAVID WINTER

Travelling light

Then Jesus called the twelve together and gave them power and authority over all demons and to cure diseases, and he sent them out to proclaim the kingdom of God and to heal. He said to them, 'Take nothing for your journey, no staff, nor bag, nor bread, nor money—not even an extra tunic. Whatever house you enter, stay there, and leave from there. Wherever they do not welcome you, as you are leaving that town shake the dust off your feet as a testimony against them.' They departed and went through the villages, bringing the good news and curing diseases everywhere.

As Jesus sent out the twelve messengers (the literal meaning of 'apostles'), whom he had chosen, he made it clear in these instructions that they were to go unencumbered. They were not to take a staff to lean on as they walked, nor bread or money or even a basic change of clothing. So, how would they manage to survive? The answer is to be found in the text. They would depend entirely on the generosity of others, learning what it means to live dependently, by grace.

In the manner of the time, they could expect, as travellers, to receive basic hospitality—somewhere to lay their mattress, as well as food and drink for the day (see also Jesus' instructions to the 'seventy' disciples in 10:7). Those who failed to offer hospitality—what Jesus calls a 'welcome'—would bring shame on their communities.

It is a picture of total commitment. The messengers of Jesus were to travel light; their call to follow Jesus would be endorsed by their own lifestyle. These words are a rebuke to comfortable Christianity, a challenge to the idea of an approach to discipleship that actually costs very little. The unencumbered life is what Jesus calls us to—not austerity for its own sake, but, nevertheless, sitting lightly to the values of the world around. In a society so often obsessed with the acquisition of 'things', his words are a bold call to us to be different.

Reflection

Those who travel light find that the journey itself is much easier.

DAVID WINTER

No easy road

Then [Jesus] said to them all, 'If any want to become my followers, let them deny themselves and take up their cross daily and follow me. For those who want to save their life will lose it, and those who lose their life for my sake will save it. What does it profit them if they gain the whole world, but lose or forfeit themselves? Those who are ashamed of me and of my words, of them the Son of Man will be ashamed when he comes in his glory and the glory of the Father and of the holy angels. But truly I tell you, there are some standing here who will not taste death before they see the kingdom of God.'

Here are some more challenging words from Jesus, this time to would-be disciples. If you want to follow me, he tells them, it will be a costly process. The rewards (hinted at here) are wonderful—the 'glory of the Father and the holy angels'—but first there is the call to commitment.

We may wonder what it means to 'deny yourself'. Surely an essential element of humanity is self-worth? After all, people go on assertiveness courses. Is Jesus saying that Christians should aspire to being nobodies, mere doormats? The clue surely is the connection between the two verbs 'deny' and 'follow': we 'deny' ourselves because we wish to 'follow'. Followers cannot simply make up their own minds where to go, because it is the leader who decides the path. So, if we wish to 'follow' Jesus, we shall, necessarily, have to deny ourselves the 'right' to go our own way. The choice, then, is then spelt out for us. On the one hand, there is the life of self, which is essentially a denial of discipleship. On the other, there is 'the kingdom of God'—the ultimate glory awaiting us at the end of the road. For some of them—three, in fact—that vision would be revealed eight days later (v. 28) when Jesus was transfigured on the holy mountain. The rest of us will have to wait!

Reflection

Self-denial on these terms is actually self-fulfilment.

DAVID WINTER

Who is the greatest?

While everyone was amazed at all that [Jesus] was doing, he said to his disciples, 'Let these words sink into your ears: the Son of Man is going to be betrayed into human hands.' But they did not understand this saying; its meaning was concealed from them, so that they could not perceive it. And they were afraid to ask him about this saying. An argument arose among them as to which one of them was the greatest. But Jesus, aware of their inner thoughts, took a little child and put it by his side, and said to them, 'Whoever welcomes this child in my name welcomes me, and whoever welcomes me welcomes the one who sent me; for the least among all of you is the greatest.'

Like stags fighting to be leader of the herd, human beings struggle over issues of status. To be Mary in the nativity play, to be head chorister, to captain the hockey team: even from our early years, too many of us enjoy being one step above the others. The disciples were no exception. Judging by the Gospel accounts, they were almost obsessively concerned with their individual status in the apostolic band. James and John even approached Jesus privately to ask that they should have the most honoured positions when he was finally 'in his glory' (Mark 10:37). Now, here, we have a public squabble on the topic—which of them is 'the greatest'—immediately after Jesus had spoken of his imminent betrayal and death. How could his close followers get it so wrong?

Church history gives us the answer. Christian ministry and the life of our churches have often been battlegrounds for issues of status. Every church member knows how easily egos are bruised when it comes to filling the various offices in a church and how hard people sometimes fight to attain that coveted position of leadership or authority.

Jesus used a small child as a visual aid in his response to the disciples' question. Whoever welcomes a child welcomes the Messiah and 'the One who sent him'. What, then, of rank?

Reflection

'The least among all of you is the greatest' (Luke 9:48).

DAVID WINTER

Not one of us

John answered, 'Master, we saw someone casting out demons in your name, and we tried to stop him, because he does not follow with us.' But Jesus said to him, 'Do not stop him; for whoever is not against you is for you.' When the days drew near for him to be taken up, he set his face to go to Jerusalem. And he sent messengers ahead of him. On their way they entered a village of the Samaritans to make ready for him; but they did not receive him, because his face was set towards Jerusalem. When his disciples James and John saw it, they said, 'Lord, do you want us to command fire to come down from heaven and consume them?' But he turned and rebuked them.

There is a well-worn joke about a new arrival in heaven being shown all its glories by an angel. They pass a high wall, from behind which come sounds of singing. 'Who's there?' the new arrival asks. 'Oh,' the angel replies, 'that's the… [here the joker inserts whichever group of religious people he rates as stand-offish and exclusive]. They think they're the only ones up here.' The trouble is, it can be true.

The disciples were bothered because someone was casting out demons in the name of Jesus (just like they were—9:1), but he was not 'one of them'. They tried to stop him and Jesus corrected them with the simple statement, 'Whoever is not against you is for you'. The label might be wrong, the authority irregular, but if this person was acting 'in the name of Jesus', then he was doing more good than harm.

A few days later, a Samaritan village did not offer welcome to Jesus. James and John were all for calling down fire from heaven to consume them, but all they got from Jesus was a rebuke. The footnote to this verse in the NRSV (with additional wording found in some ancient texts) explains his reaction: 'The Son of Man has not come to destroy the lives of human beings, but to save them.'

Reflection

Perhaps the day will come when the only 'label' we shall need is 'Christian'.

DAVID WINTER

The true disciple

As they were going along the road, someone said to him, 'I will follow you wherever you go.' And Jesus said to him, 'Foxes have holes, and birds of the air have nests; but the Son of Man has nowhere to lay his head.' To another he said, 'Follow me.' But he said, 'Lord, first let me go and bury my father.' But Jesus said to him, 'Let the dead bury their own dead; but as for you, go and proclaim the kingdom of God.' Another said, 'I will follow you, Lord; but let me first say farewell to those at my home.' Jesus said to him, 'No one who puts a hand to the plough and looks back is fit for the kingdom of God.'

Sometimes there is a significant key word in a passage. Here, it is the tiny two-letter Greek preposition *de*, meaning 'but' or 'on the other hand'. It occurs six times in these six sentences. In fact, each of the would-be disciples is saying, in effect, 'Lord, I will follow you, but...'. They want discipleship without commitment; they feel an attraction to the leader without a willingness to follow unconditionally. Most of us have probably tried being disciples and found out that, with Jesus, it really does mean everything or nothing.

The first would-be disciple sounds promising with his bold words, 'I will follow wherever you go'. Jesus simply points out that following him will be costly and uncomfortable, and that seems to have punctured the bubble of enthusiasm. The second aspirant responds positively, but puts in a delaying factor—'first let me bury my father'. That sounds reasonable enough, but the phrase as used at the time usually meant 'after my father has died, when I have got my inheritance'. He is soon corrected by Jesus and shown that he must get his priorities right. So must the third would-be follower, who agrees to follow, but only after he or she has said farewell to the family, which could have meant a dozen sets of relatives and taken weeks to do. The call was to follow *now*!

Reflection
You cannot follow by looking back over your shoulder.

DAVID WINTER

Welcoming the stranger

The theme of the Women's World Day of Prayer this year (8 March) is 'I was a stranger and you welcomed me'. These well-known words of Jesus are from his parable, recorded in Matthew 25:35, and his charge to us to welcome strangers is consistent with other teaching that runs throughout the Bible.

Being a stranger can be unnerving, particularly when others around us seem to belong in a way that we do not. We may have the experience of being in a foreign country where others speak a language that we do not understand and behave in ways that feel alien to us. Maybe we visit another church where they do things very differently and all appear to know each other well, so we may feel alienated in the very place we had hoped to find a sense of belonging. We can have ambivalent feelings about strangers: if someone turns up and is different from us, that difference can make us anxious and feel on our guard.

As we think about this theme in the coming two weeks, we will use Bible passages to reflect on who these 'strangers' might be for us and what kind of hospitality the scriptures urge us to offer them. We live in a world marked by terrible suffering and pain because people have been unable to live with those who are different. We look with dismay at the conflicts and dreadful waste of life where people have not only failed to welcome strangers but also made enemies of them. Most of us reading these notes will not be in those sharp places of conflict, but we may well find ourselves close to those who feel, for one reason or another, strangers in the community because of skin colour, family or economic situation, sexual orientation, personal beliefs and convictions and a whole host of other factors that can stand in the way of friendship. As we shall see, the Bible is clear that we are called to welcome strangers, not avoid them or be hostile to them. The comforting aspect of this is that, in those times when we feel estranged from our fellow men and women, God's heart is with us.

Michael Mitton

Dark promises

As the sun was going down, a deep sleep fell upon Abram, and a deep and terrifying darkness descended upon him. Then the Lord said to Abram, 'Know this for certain, that your offspring shall be aliens in a land that is not theirs, and shall be slaves there, and they shall be oppressed for four hundred years; but I will bring judgment on the nation that they serve, and afterward they shall come out with great possessions.'

Abraham (Abram) was from Mesopotamia and there, at the age of 75, he heard God's call to journey to Canaan. When he and his family first arrived there, they surely must have felt like strangers and, no doubt, the local people would have looked on them with suspicion. Abraham, however, trusted that this was the land where his descendants would settle. In today's passage, though, a terrible darkness comes over him and, in that dark place, he heard a word from God promising a 400-year future of alienation and slavery. Even though the prophecy included assurances of eventually settling in the land (15:16–21), less comforting words are hard to imagine. The destiny of Abraham's people was to include a time of estrangement in the land of Egypt.

We may well wonder why God thought it necessary to let his people experience such a long period of being strangers in a foreign land and not just strangers but also slaves. What was in the divine mind, in the promising of a homeland, but then trapping several generations of his people far from that homeland? In time it becomes clear that this time of estrangement did have a purpose. It proved how deep the longing for the promised land lay in the hearts of the people. Further, it gave them a first-hand experience of what it was like to be a stranger in someone else's land so that compassion for strangers would dwell deep in their souls. Times of darkness and estrangement can be painful, but they can also be times when we discover the depths of our longings and grow in compassion.

Prayer

Lord, when darkness overshadows my soul, keep my hope firm and deepen my compassion.

MICHAEL MITTON

EXODUS 22:21–24

God's feelings for strangers

You shall not wrong or oppress a resident alien, for you were aliens in the land of Egypt. You shall not abuse any widow or orphan. If you do abuse them, when they cry out to me, I will surely heed their cry; my wrath will burn, and I will kill you with the sword, and your wives shall become widows and your children orphans.

In the end, it was just *over* 400 years that the people of God resided as aliens in Egypt, until Moses led them on that long journey back to the promised land. Though a desert journey, it was a very fertile time in other ways, especially in terms of receiving God's laws and teaching. Today's passage is an instruction regarding attitudes to strangers and revealing God's feelings about those who are marginalised.

There is always something shocking and uncomfortable about this kind of reading, in which God threatens to burn with wrath and kill people, but it is important to catch the profound message that this kind of strong language is trying to convey. In this case, the message is: if God is driven to such distress that he is even considering ending the very lives he has created, he must feel strongly about the matter. The matter in question is the care of strangers and others who feel alienated because of terrible misfortunes.

Anyone who feels like a stranger, in whatever context, should take comfort from this passage, because it reveals the depth of God's feelings for them. In this passage, the groups of marginalised people whom God speaks about are those who are resident aliens (people from other nations and cultures, who would feel very different from the native population) and widows and orphans (those who have lost people very close to them, who feel alone and vulnerable as a result). God's heart is clearly with these people. If his heart is with them, then ours need to be with them, too.

Reflection

If you feel like a stranger in some situation today, remember how God feels about you. Are there ways in which you can show God's compassion to a stranger today?

MICHAEL MITTON

The command to love strangers

You shall not strip your vineyard bare, or gather the fallen grapes of your vineyard; you shall leave them for the poor and the alien: I am the Lord your God... When an alien resides with you in your land, you shall not oppress the alien. The alien who resides with you shall be to you as the citizen among you; you shall love the alien as yourself, for you were aliens in the land of Egypt: I am the Lord your God.

This message, which is reiterated in other passages in Exodus, Leviticus and Deuteronomy, is a clear and simple one: it is that strangers are to be welcomed and not treated in a hostile way. The reasoning, often given in these passages, is that the people of God were themselves once aliens, so they should know what it is like to suffer in this way. Their story of suffering should inspire compassion for those similarly afflicted.

Leviticus 19 is an expanded form of the Ten Commandments, so this instruction to care for strangers is right at the centre of how God wants his people to behave. We are commanded to love our neighbours and there may well be times when those neighbours are, in one way or another, strangers.

Messages are often repeated when people find it hard to hear them or stubbornly refuse to listen to them and, indeed, history has shown how we have often found it very difficult to live alongside those who are different from us. Humans can instinctively feel anxious in the presence of those who are different. Racial prejudice is just one obvious expression of this anxiety, but, as we read passages like today's, it is clear that God's people are commanded to be at the forefront of welcoming those who are different, foreign or feel alienated in any way. The Bible is unequivocal on this matter—the people of God are called to be a welcoming people and instinctively help strangers to feel at home.

Prayer

Lord, help me to hear and obey your commandments and may such obedience lead me to welcome a stranger today.

MICHAEL MITTON

A story of welcome: Ruth

But Ruth said, 'Do not press me to leave you or to turn back from following you! Where you go, I will go; where you lodge, I will lodge; your people shall be my people, and your God my God. Where you die, I will die—there will I be buried. May the Lord do thus and so to me, and more as well, if even death parts me from you!'

Ruth was a young woman from Moab, which lay on the other side of the Dead Sea from Judah. Although her story is set in a time of temporary peace, hostility between the two nations had been severe, with atrocities committed by both sides. A famine in Judah had driven Elimelech to take his wife Naomi and two sons to Moab, where they would have lived as strangers. The sons married Moabite women, one of them being Ruth. Disaster strikes as the three men die and the desolate Naomi returns to Bethlehem. Because of her devotion to Naomi, Ruth leaves her homeland and, in the relationship between these two women, we see a wonderful example of reconciliation between two nationalities.

Both know what it is to live as aliens in the other's country and, in their bereavements, they discover a power of love that transcends ancient enmity. The story develops further as the Israelite Boaz falls in love with the Moabite Ruth and, although it was in accordance with the law, no doubt some disapproved of his marrying a Moabite. The book ends with a brief genealogy showing that the child born to this couple is none other than the grandfather of the great King David and, therefore, an ancestor of Jesus.

There is something very moving about the way Naomi and Ruth step out of patterns of enmity into a new, healed order. As you read their story, you sense that these lives influence many others. Maybe this is one reason this book is so important: it shows how the choices that apparently ordinary people make can have huge effects. For those of us who think we live ordinary lives, it stands as a challenge and a hope.

Prayer

Lord, give me the courage to choose your ways.

Michael Mitton

A story of welcome: Mephibosheth

Mephibosheth son of Jonathan son of Saul came to David, and fell on his face and did obeisance. David said, 'Mephibosheth!' He answered, 'I am your servant.' David said to him, 'Do not be afraid, for I will show you kindness for the sake of your father Jonathan; I will restore to you all the land of your grandfather Saul, and you yourself shall eat at my table always.' He did obeisance and said, 'What is your servant, that you should look upon a dead dog such as I?'

Mephibosheth was the son of Jonathan and grandson of Saul. He was five years old when his father and grandfather fell in the battle of Mount Gilboa. Hearing of this calamity, his nurse fled with him from Gibeah, the royal residence, and, in her haste, stumbled, dropping him on the ground and causing his paralysis (2 Samuel 4:4). He was carried to the land of Gilead and stayed in a place called Lo Debar (meaning 'no pasture') until David called for him.

Many kings would have viewed Mephibosheth as a threat. Although he was the son of David's much-loved friend Jonathan, he was also the grandson of the previous king and any wanting to usurp David might well have seen an opportunity in Mephibosheth, but David's honour and mercy are stronger than his fears. Mephibosheth evidently felt awkward in David's presence and used very derogatory language about himself. He may also have felt a sense of estrangement as he was disabled and it is likely that, in the prevailing culture, not many viewed his disability with compassion. David is welcoming, however, and judges him neither by his past nor by his disability. It is his love for his father that drives his desire to welcome Mephibosheth.

Many of our responses in life are driven by either fear or love. This story is one in which love wins over fear. For Mephibosheth, David's welcome brought him from a place of 'no pasture' to a royal table. In this way, David models God's welcome to us.

Reflection

What does this story say to situations you may find yourself in, where you are anxious about a person or people?

MICHAEL MITTON

Aliens in the messianic age

So you shall divide this land among you according to the tribes of Israel. You shall allot it as an inheritance for yourselves and for the aliens who reside among you and have begotten children among you. They shall be to you as citizens of Israel; with you they shall be allotted an inheritance among the tribes of Israel. In whatever tribe aliens reside, there you shall assign them their inheritance, says the Lord God.

After his call in 593BC, Ezekiel prophesied to the people of God before and during the time of the exile in Babylon. He was entrusted with messages of judgment to the people in and around Jerusalem before its destruction by Nebuchadnezzar, then journeyed with his people into exile, where he then delivered messages of hope to a very forlorn people.

Ezekiel was a priest and, therefore, very familiar with the temple. A number of his visions centre on the temple and today's passage is one such vision, coming towards the end of his book. In it, Ezekiel sees water gushing out through the door of the temple and becoming a deep river of blessing that waters a new promised land where there are to be no strangers. Today's passage could not be clearer: in the new world for which God is preparing his people, the strangers and aliens will be so welcomed that they will be as one with the citizens of Israel.

Centuries later, John, writing the book of Revelation, heard a similar message. He saw a vision of a great multitude of people 'from every nation, from all tribes and peoples and languages' standing before the throne of God (Revelation 7:9).

The prophets in the scriptures who peered into the far-distant future saw most clearly that the eventual kingdom of God is one where no one is a stranger and all anxieties about differences have been healed. These insights into our future not only give us hope that at the end of this age there will be peace and justice but also inspire us to usher in such changes to our world now.

Prayer

Lord, may your kingdom come on earth, as in heaven.

Michael Mitton

The magi

In the time of King Herod, after Jesus was born in Bethlehem of Judea, wise men from the East came to Jerusalem, asking, 'Where is the child who has been born king of the Jews? For we observed his star at its rising, and have come to pay him homage.'... On entering the house, they saw the child with Mary his mother; and they knelt down and paid him homage.

Matthew starts and finishes his Gospel with one clear message: God is with us. In the first chapter (v. 23), he quotes Isaiah—'"they shall name him Emmanuel", which means "God is with us"'—and he closes with the words of Jesus—'I am with you always, to the end of the age' (28:20). The question the reader might then ask is 'Who is "us"?'

Matthew makes clear right at the start that the 'us' in question is a far broader group than many would expect. No sooner has he quoted this passage from Isaiah at the opening of his Gospel, than he introduces us to the magi—that curious group of men who travelled to Judea from the East. They came as national and cultural strangers into a land and religion that had little space for their way of thinking.

Matthew tells this story to show that God, who has come to earth as a human, is here for *all* of us, regardless of whether we are 'in' or 'out' by human reckoning. Welcoming strangers is such an important theme in the heart of God, that he called these foreigners to meet Jesus right at the start of his life on earth. Icons of the magi visiting Christ invariably include the child raising his hand in blessing to these foreigners and though, of course, we do not really know his response to these visitors, the impression you get is certainly that they were most welcome. When we come across those who have different faiths and beliefs from ours, it is good to remember the welcome given to these magi by the Christ-child. Welcoming does not mean condoning others' beliefs: it creates space for Jesus to make his presence felt.

Reflection
Who are today's 'magi'?

MICHAEL MITTON

72

Loving the enemy

'You have heard that it was said, "You shall love your neighbour and hate your enemy." But I say to you, love your enemies and pray for those who persecute you, so that you may be children of your Father in heaven; for he makes his sun rise on the evil and on the good, and sends rain on the righteous and on the unrighteous. For if you love those who love you, what reward do you have? Do not even the tax collectors do the same?'

When Jesus first spoke these words, his audience would have had little difficulty in thinking of who it was that threatened them: most of them probably thought of the Romans. In a situation of political or national conflict, the enemy is obvious, but the concept of the enemy is not just confined to such situations. Every one of us can have enemies, even if we do not describe them as such. Anyone who threatens us can make us feel very uncomfortable. Conflicts happen all the time between people with differing personalities, values and beliefs. Others annoy and irritate us for many different reasons and though we may be reluctant to class them as 'enemies', they nonetheless can threaten our peace. We may handle such situations by being rather cold in our responses or trying to pretend it does not exist or becoming aggressive. Jesus' teaching makes it clear that none of these responses is a Christian option. His call is to reach out in love to the person who threatens us and to pray for him or her.

'Strangers' we are called to welcome may not be of a different colour, culture or religion from our own. They may actually be people from whom we are estranged in some way. They may even be so distant from us that they are seen as 'enemies', thereby threatening us in some way. Today's words from Jesus, therefore, are among his most difficult and radical, but obeying commands like these has the power to transform relationships and even change nations.

Reflection

Who is your 'enemy'? Is there anything you can do today
to 'love your enemies'?

MICHAEL MITTON

Jesus the foreigner

Jesus left that place and went away to the district of Tyre and Sidon. Just then a Canaanite woman from that region came out and started shouting, 'Have mercy on me, Lord, Son of David; my daughter is tormented by a demon.' But he did not answer her at all. And his disciples came and urged him, saying, 'Send her away, for she keeps shouting after us.'

Today's passage is from a story that takes place in the region of Tyre and Sidon, an area much more influenced by Greek than Jewish culture. The cities were centres of paganism, with temples to gods such as Heracles and Astarte. Jesus, as a Jewish rabbi from Galilee, would have been seen as a foreigner, so this episode is special because it is one of the few where Jesus is the stranger in a foreign land and culture. While many would have treated him and his followers with the usual suspicions and anxiety, there is one person who does not and it is the Canaanite woman, whose child is tormented by a demon. Perhaps it is her desperation that causes her to cross the cultural boundaries and cry out to Jesus for help. Maybe she is just naturally impatient with such divisions.

Initially, Jesus appears to conform to national and religious stereotype and does not respond to the woman, but she is determined to break through, for she is convinced that this foreigner can cure her child. It is her faith that so impresses Jesus and, once he sees it shining from her beseeching face, he delivers her daughter from oppression. In fact, the whole story turns on the woman's faith, which releases the healing (v. 28). Perhaps more significantly, it is faith that dismantles the cultural barriers, to the extent that no one is a stranger by the end of the episode.

Christians can often feel strangers in the secular context of our age, but here Jesus models for us a wonderful confidence in entering a different world, spotting signs of faith and doing the works of the kingdom.

Prayer

Lord give me the eyes to see signs of faith in the people around me and to be open to your wonders.

MICHAEL MITTON

From Babel to Pentecost

Now there were devout Jews from every nation under heaven living in Jerusalem. And at this sound the crowd gathered and was bewildered, because each one heard them speaking in the native language of each. Amazed and astonished, they asked, 'Are not all these who are speaking Galileans? And how is it that we hear, each of us, in our own native language?'

The story of Pentecost has often been contrasted with the story of the tower of Babel (Genesis 11:1–9). In the Babel story, people try to reach up to God by building a massive tower and, as a punishment for their pride, they are scattered across the face of the earth, speaking a host of different languages. In the Pentecost story, God the Holy Spirit visits a group of people humbly at prayer and he releases a language gift among them so that visitors from all over the known world can understand them.

The first story is about alienation and the second about community. In the first story, people who were once friends become strangers to each other. In the second story, those who come to Jerusalem as strangers meet a people who speak their language and make them feel at home so that they are no longer strangers. Acts 2 ends with the story of the new community that is formed in Jerusalem and, far from them being scattered, 'the Lord added to their number' (vv. 43–47).

Many of the gifts of the Spirit listed by Paul in 1 Corinthians 12 are 'for the common good' (v. 7) and the whole thrust of this chapter and chapter 13 following is that the Spirit is this divine community-builder, releasing extraordinary love into the disciples of Jesus. With this in mind, no one should feel a stranger in church. The sad truth is that many do. Where we have become aware of people who feel estranged and alienated in our churches, perhaps we should pray with greater conviction 'Come, Holy Spirit' and look not for sensational gifts, but for the growth of real community.

Reflection

How does the Holy Spirit help you to 'speak the language' of others?

Michael Mitton

GALATIANS 3:26–29

The abolition of divisions

For in Christ Jesus you are all children of God through faith. As many of you as were baptised into Christ have clothed yourselves with Christ. There is no longer Jew or Greek, there is no longer slave or free, there is no longer male and female; for all of you are one in Christ Jesus. And if you belong to Christ, then you are Abraham's offspring, heirs according to the promise.

In today's passage, Paul looks back to Abraham—the one who made that epic journey of faith to a strange land and began the great community of faith. Paul teaches that, as children of Abraham, we are part of the new community of faith and, in this community, the divisions between Jew and Greek, slave and free, male and female are broken down. In his discussion of the Spirit in 1 Corinthians 12, he also makes reference to this dismantling of painful divisions between people (v. 13), as we are baptised by one Spirit into one body.

The three divisions that Paul comments on are ones that have plagued human relationships for centuries. 'Jew and Greek' speaks of religious and cultural differences; 'slave and free' speaks of economic and social differences; 'male and female' speaks of gender differences.

In 1906, William Seymour, a black preacher from a very poor background, found himself at the epicentre of an outpouring of the Holy Spirit that became the birth of the worldwide Pentecostal movement. What particularly thrilled Seymour was that cultural, social and gender divides collapsed as the Holy Spirit graced those early meetings. It was not uncommon to find poor black women ministering to wealthy white men. Sadly, other white male leaders of the movement did not share this vision of unity.

The Holy Spirit is to guide us into truth (John 16:13), and all of us need his searchlight in our hearts to show us if we have made strangers of others because they are from a different culture, class or gender to us. It can be disturbing to discover pockets of prejudice in our souls, but wonderfully liberating to be relieved of them.

Prayer

Lord, if there is prejudice in my heart, then show me, I pray.

MICHAEL MITTON

Entertaining angels unaware

Let mutual love continue. Do not neglect to show hospitality to strangers, for by doing that some have entertained angels without knowing it. Remember those who are in prison, as though you were in prison with them; those who are being tortured, as though you yourselves were being tortured. Let marriage be held in honour by all, and let the marriage bed be kept undefiled; for God will judge fornicators and adulterers. Keep your lives free from the love of money, and be content with what you have; for he has said, 'I will never leave you or forsake you.'

However we are meant to understand this entertaining of angels without knowing it, the writer here urges us to greet strangers with a sense of expectation. The core message is that a stranger, whom we might scarcely notice, has the potential to share with us a message from God.

This opens us to new possibilities. Anyone we pass in the street, sit beside on a bus, wait behind in a queue or open a door to could be an 'angel'. Maybe, like Manoah and his wife in Judges 13, we will encounter an angel in disguise, but what is certain is that God may use any stranger to be a bearer of his message to us. Hospitality, in this context, is about our showing an open and welcoming heart to strangers, acknowledging that they may have more to give us than we have to give them.

In the next verse of today's passage, the writer invites us to remember prisoners. It feels like an extraordinary leap, but, once we start opening our hearts to the possibility that strangers can be messengers of God, we may well find that the messages we hear open us up to caring for those, such as prisoners, who are so estranged from others.

The writer also touches on the threats to marriage, where the closest friendship is to be enjoyed, and the danger of money that has made strangers out of too many people.

The final verse assures us that God will never view any of us as strangers.

Reflection

Who has been an 'angel' to you recently?
Who could you be an 'angel' to today?

MICHAEL MITTON

I was a stranger and you welcomed me

'Then the king will say to those at his right hand, "Come, you that are blessed by my Father, inherit the kingdom prepared for you from the foundation of the world; for I was hungry and you gave me food, I was thirsty and you gave me something to drink, I was a stranger and you welcomed me, I was naked and you gave me clothing, I was sick and you took care of me, I was in prison and you visited me."'

Today's passage is part of the parable of the sheep and the goats used by Jesus to teach how God will judge his people. In this parable, where God is pictured as a king, one group of people is commended by the king for showing great kindness to him. When the recipients of this praise show surprise, the king replies, 'as you did it to one of the least of these who are members of my family, you did it to me' (v. 40). There is a corresponding shock for those who are castigated by the king for not showing this level of kindness to his family (vv. 41–46).

As we have been looking at the theme of welcoming strangers these past two weeks, it will not surprise you to find that Jesus includes 'a stranger' in the list of those to be cared for in this world. What is perhaps surprising, though, is that Jesus identifies so closely with strangers, as he does with the hungry, naked and so on. Each time we reach out in hospitality to a stranger, it is not just an angel that we might be entertaining unawares, but God himself. No doubt Jesus could see the real danger of people spiritualising their love for God, the idea that 'all we have to do is a few religious things and God will be impressed'. What this passage teaches with fierce clarity is that our love for God has to be expressed by loving our fellow humans, particularly those who are in need, including strangers. To fail to do this carries the very real risk of being estranged from God.

Prayer

Lord, sharpen the eyesight of my heart, that I may see you
in the strangers I meet.

MICHAEL MITTON

Stranger on the shore

Just after daybreak, Jesus stood on the beach; but the disciples did not know that it was Jesus. Jesus said to them, 'Children, you have no fish, have you?' They answered him, 'No.' He said to them, 'Cast the net to the right side of the boat, and you will find some.' So they cast it, and now they were not able to haul it in because there were so many fish. That disciple whom Jesus loved said to Peter, 'It is the Lord!'

A curious feature of the resurrected Jesus was that even those who had known him very well in his earthly life failed at first to recognise him (Mary Magdalene in John 20:11–18 and Cleopas in Luke 24:13–35). Similarly, in today's story, several of the apostles are out fishing when they are beckoned by this stranger on the shore who offers some helpful fishing advice. When they haul in a miraculous catch, they recognise him and Peter leaps into the water to reach him.

There are times in our Christian lives when it can feel as if the Jesus we have known so well becomes something of a stranger. We can go through a wilderness time, spiritually, and all our usual devices to draw us close to him, such as prayer, Bible reading and worship, seem to have little effect. This can sometimes be because we have to discover something new about Jesus. It is as if he has deliberately become a stranger to us so that we have to find him again and, in so doing, find out new things about him. When Peter realised that the stranger on the shore was in fact Jesus, he rushed to greet him. Jesus then takes him to one side and, in the conversation that follows (21:15–23), there is a tender discussion about love, life and death. There are moments when Jesus appears to be a stranger, but such times often herald a new closeness to him and a new word for our hearts.

Prayer

Lord, even when you appear as a stranger, your love reaches out to me. Call me afresh today and open my heart to your words of life.

MICHAEL MITTON

Jesus' wisdom in Luke

The opening verses of the book of Psalms (1:1–3) sums up the biblical understanding of wisdom rather well: 'Happy are those who do not follow the advice of the wicked, or take the path that sinners tread, or sit in the seat of scoffers; but their delight is in the law of the Lord… They are like trees planted by streams of water, which yield their fruit in due season.'

Wisdom is not just something acquired by hard work (though it is hard). It is not the same as cleverness or knowledge; it comes from being rooted in the right ground. For the Old Testament tradition, this is chiefly about God's law. By meditating on God's law, by being rooted in it, people would be wise. For us Christians, the law and wisdom of God are embodied in Jesus, so we need to root ourselves in him. 'Abide in me', like branches of a vine, says Jesus (John 15:4–5).

We still have much to learn from the Old Testament, but we can also see that it points us to Jesus. The streams of water where we can plant ourselves and bear fruit are the waters of baptism. As we are incorporated into the church, which is Christ's body here on earth, we begin to receive from him and, over a lifetime of discipleship, we begin to embody the wisdom of God as we see it in Christ. This is true holiness: the Holy Spirit revealing in us the beauty and goodness of Jesus Christ.

'Trust in the Lord with all your heart, and do not rely on your own insight', says that other Old Testament book of wisdom, Proverbs (3:5). Of all the gifts that we receive in the church, the one that will help us the most to grow in wisdom is the scriptures. The Bible itself is a stream of living water. Chapters 10—12 of Luke's Gospel contain much of Jesus' own teaching. By dwelling in them through this next fortnight, we can learn from God and refine our discipleship so that Christ will be alive in us. Like trees planted in streams of water, we will bear fruit for God.

Stephen Cottrell

LUKE 10:38–42

The better part

As they went on their way, [Jesus] entered a certain village, where a woman named Martha welcomed him into her home. She had a sister named Mary, who sat at the Lord's feet and listened to what he was saying. But Martha was distracted by her many tasks; so she came to him and asked, 'Lord, do you not care that my sister has left me to do all the work by myself? Tell her then to help me.' But the Lord answered her, 'Martha, Martha, you are worried and distracted by many things; there is need of only one thing. Mary has chosen the better part, which will not be taken away from her.'

Be honest: is there anyone who hasn't occasionally found this story a little irritating? Of course Mary has chosen the better part—Jesus says so—but we still have a sneaking sympathy for Martha. While her sister sits at Jesus' feet, she does all the work! Most of us can think of occasions where we have been the Martha and have looked with thinly veiled exasperation at rather too many people who, casting themselves in the role of Mary, have failed to pull their weight. So, let's get this clear from the beginning: there is work to be done and Jesus does not mean that we should sit around in prayer and contemplation while others do our share. We need Marthas *and* Marys and we must each discover the Martha and the Mary inside ourselves.

There is a time for everything, says the book of Ecclesiastes (3:1–8): a time for work, a time for rest and a time for prayer. Wisdom is about staying close to Jesus in all three. We need to make Jesus our guide, not Mary. She does the right thing in this situation, but so does Martha in others. After all, it is Martha who welcomes Jesus into the house in the first place. Let us welcome Jesus into our lives through these scriptures that we shall be exploring together and learn wisdom for our daily lives.

Prayer

Holy Spirit, guide my life this week. Enable me to stay close to Jesus and to learn his wisdom for my life.

STEPHEN COTTRELL

Lord, teach us to pray

[Jesus] was praying in a certain place, and after he had finished, one of his disciples said to him, 'Lord, teach us to pray, as John taught his disciples.' He said to them, 'When you pray, say: "Father, hallowed be your name. Your kingdom come."'

'Teach us to pray.' That is what the disciples ask Jesus and it is where Christian wisdom begins and ends. 'The fear of the Lord is the beginning of knowledge' (Proverbs 1:7). We learn this fear and knowledge of God when we live our lives in communion with God, which is nurtured by prayer, a prayer that is made possible by what God has done for us in Jesus Christ. He is the one in whom we pray; he is the one who teaches us the way of prayer. Prayer is God's work in us.

So, Jesus teaches his friends. He says to them, 'Pray like this': 'Father, hallowed be your name. Your kingdom come', though in the version of the Lord's Prayer from Matthew's Gospel (the one we may say ourselves each day), Jesus also adds 'Your will be done' (Matthew 6:10). These three together—holding God's name holy, seeking God's will and working for God's kingdom—are the heart of prayer. It is not about feverishly hectoring God with all the stuff we think he should be attending to, but about giving him honour and praise, seeking his will for our lives and for the world and using the words of Jesus to shape our mind and will.

Prayer is not just intercession. It is not about our trying to change God's mind. It is praise and adoration. It is about being open to God changing ours. This is the way of Christian wisdom.

We can do no better than making the Lord's Prayer our prayer. Many great spiritual writers have commented that if we could just say the Lord's Prayer once, really meaning it, then we would be holy. Give it a try; it will take a lifetime, but, by happy coincidence, that's exactly how much time each of us has.

Prayer

Jesus, teach me to pray. Teach me your prayer and do your will in me.

STEPHEN COTTRELL

Give us what we need

'Give us each day our daily bread; And forgive us our sins, for we ourselves forgive everyone indebted to us. And do not bring us to the time of trial.'

Once we have prayer round the right way, then life is round the right way. First of all, prayer is not about what we say to God, it is about what God says to us. Thus, it begins with the hearty praises we offer to God in the first three clauses of the Lord's Prayer. In the rightness and the goodness of this relationship we can then ask God anything. So it is that the Lord's Prayer continues with three humble petitions where we ask God for our most basic needs—provision for each day, sins to be forgiven (and the grace to forgive others) and for God to save us from the time of trial.

Once again, we find that Jesus' own words enable us not just to say the prayer but also to discover what we really want. Other spiritual writers have said that our own deepest desire is the will of God. The trouble is that most of the time we are not aware of what we truly want—we are only aware of ourselves at a very superficial level—but this prayer reveals what we really need and shapes our deepest longings.

We live in a world that always wants more. We are imprisoned by our own possessions and our obsession with getting more. We nurse grievances and grudges against our neighbours. Meanwhile, so many of our current economic woes are caused by debt on a grand scale and an inability to share with others. In a world of plenty, millions still starve. The problem is simple: we do not know the wisdom of God. We put ourselves first. We expect too much. We ask for what we do not need.

What a different world it would be if we could simply learn to ask for daily bread, daily forgiveness and nothing more, then be satisfied with it.

Prayer

God, give me what I need and save me from asking or craving for more.
Forgive me and help me to forgive others.

Stephen Cottrell

Persevere

[Jesus] said to them, 'Suppose one of you has a friend, and you go to him at midnight and say to him, "Friend, lend me three loaves of bread; for a friend of mine has arrived, and I have nothing to set before him." And he answers from within, "Do not bother me; the door has already been locked, and my children are with me in bed; I cannot get up and give you anything." I tell you, even though he will not get up and give him anything because he is his friend, at least because of his persistence he will get up and give him whatever he needs. So I say to you, ask, and it will be given to you; search, and you will find; knock, and the door will be opened for you.'

The wisdom of Jesus comes through stories as much as sayings. Many of what we today call parables could just as easily be called riddles or puzzles. They need to be worked out; each answer leads to another question. There is never a point where you can say, 'I've got it now'. That is because, ultimately, the wisdom of Jesus is Jesus himself. Remember the first words of the Lord's Prayer? 'Our Father'. That is not God as we expected. Instead, he is a Father to us; he is ours; we can have relationship with him.

That relationship is made possible through Jesus and this is the greatest wisdom of Christian scripture: Jesus is not just a teacher, not just a philosopher; he is God's wisdom enfleshed. So, as this playful little story puts it, be persistent. Ask. Search. Knock. This wisdom is instantly available through relationship with God in Jesus. You do need to work at it, but receiving it is not dependent on your work. It is given freely: 'received in one great gulp of grace' as the third-century saint Cyprian of Carthage put it. What you need to do is work out what it means for your life. That is the subject of a lifetime's learning. There will always be more to know and apply.

Prayer

Jesus, help me to persevere in the school of your love
that I might learn from you.

STEPHEN COTTRELL

Asking for the right things

'Is there anyone among you who, if your child asks for a fish, will give a snake instead of a fish? Or if the child asks for an egg, will give a scorpion? If you then, who are evil, know how to give good gifts to your children, how much more will the heavenly Father give the Holy Spirit to those who ask him!'

We return again to the issue of asking for the right things, having our will refined. This is a point Jesus wants to labour. God knows you; God wants to give you what you need. Wisdom comes from him, so stop looking in the wrong places. Stop asking for the wrong things.

Unfortunately, what we need is not always the same as what we want. We do not always ask for fish or eggs: sometimes snakes and scorpions seem rather more beguiling. We hanker after what we should not have, what we know to be wrong. Sin is compelling and attractive; they do not call it temptation for nothing. If there were not so many seductions at hand, being chaste would be easy, fidelity a cinch.

If we allow ourselves to be shaped by God's wisdom, we will learn to desire and ask for the right things. This will not happen quickly or easily—it is part of that lifetime of discipleship where our stubborn wills are slowly shaped so that they conform to the will of God. As Jesus says, 'If you then, who are evil, know how to give good gifts to your children, how much more will the heavenly Father give the Holy Spirit to those who ask him!' (v. 13). That is the other great promise of the Christian faith: God will give us the Spirit, which is what we need more than anything, because it is what will bring and instil the wisdom of Jesus in our lives. It will be God's work in us, his gift to us. The Spirit will bring forgiveness, perseverance, patience, self-control. With these we will learn what is good for us.

Prayer

Heavenly Father, show me what I need and help me to desire it. Give me the Spirit so that I may grow in the way of Christ.

STEPHEN COTTRELL

Saying yes to God

> While [Jesus] was saying this, a woman in the crowd raised her voice and said to him, 'Blessed is the womb that bore you and the breasts that nursed you!' But he said, 'Blessed rather are those who hear the word of God and obey it!'

Sometimes this passage can be read as Jesus giving his mother a bit of a putdown. Far from it! Jesus says that the one who is blessed is the one who hears the word of God and obeys it. If there is one person who exemplifies this obedience it is Mary, for, right at the beginning of the Gospel story in Luke (1:38), she is the one who responds to the angel's strange and disturbing offer with absolute faithfulness: 'Here am I, the servant of the Lord; let it be with me according to your word'. Her cousin Elizabeth says of her, 'Blessed is she who believed that there would be a fulfilment of what was spoken to her by the Lord' (v. 45). In other words, Mary is blessed not just because she bore the Christ but also because she 'hears the word of God and obeys it'.

We could go further and say that without her cooperation with the will of God, the Christ could not have come. God does not force himself on anyone, certainly not the virgin Mary and not in the incarnation. Heaven waits on earth's response, and Mary's 'Yes' to God was the turning point of human history.

It is the same today. God will not force himself on any of us. He waits for our response and we are blessed not because of any earthly mark of upbringing or pedigree (God is not impressed by our estimates of greatness), but because we too hear and respond to God's word and, by doing so, are incorporated into God's household. It is our being united with God's will that makes us part of God's family, brothers and sisters of Christ. Mary is therefore a model of Christian discipleship, one who teaches us how to receive and bear the wisdom of God that is Jesus Christ.

Prayer

Heavenly Father, like Mary, teach me to say 'Yes' to your word.

STEPHEN COTTRELL

Turning around

When the crowds were increasing, [Jesus] began to say, 'This generation is an evil generation; it asks for a sign, but no sign will be given to it except the sign of Jonah. For just as Jonah became a sign to the people of Nineveh, so the Son of Man will be to this generation. The queen of the South will rise at the judgment with the people of this generation and condemn them, because she came from the ends of the earth to listen to the wisdom of Solomon, and see, something greater than Solomon is here! The people of Nineveh will rise up at the judgment with this generation and condemn it, because they repented at the proclamation of Jonah, and see, something greater than Jonah is here!'

An obvious next question is, 'What do we do to receive this wisdom?' The answer is paradoxical. It cannot be earned or learned; it arises from our relationship with God. It is a free gift, but it must be consciously received, unwrapped and applied. That takes a lifetime of learning, which is where repentance comes in. Repentance is not the precondition for receiving God's wisdom, but it is a very necessary part of our ongoing response to God, whereby his image and likeness—his wisdom and his ways—are formed in us. 'The people of Nineveh will rise up at the judgment with this generation and condemn it, because they repented at the proclamation of Jonah', says Jesus, 'and see, something greater than Jonah is here!' (v. 32). That which is greater than Jonah is the presence of Jesus himself who is not just the one who calls us to repentance, but also the one through whom we are forgiven and reconciled to God.

The biblical word for repentance is *metanoia*—literally, 'turned around'. It is not just saying sorry for the things we do wrong, but a complete reorientation of life. Once we see the wisdom of God's way, we cannot help but recognise the waywardness of our own. That is the wisdom which is greater than Solomon's. It is not about our own insightful cleverness, but joyful obedience to God's directing.

Prayer

Holy Spirit, redirect me.

STEPHEN COTTRELL

Let there be light

Jesus said, 'No one after lighting a lamp puts it in a cellar, but on the lampstand so that those who enter may see the light. Your eye is the lamp of your body. If your eye is healthy, your whole body is full of light; but if it is not healthy, your body is full of darkness. Therefore consider whether the light in you is not darkness. If then your whole body is full of light, with no part of it in darkness, it will be as full of light as when a lamp gives you light with its rays.'

The image of a brightly burning lamp was much more powerful to a world without electricity. We take light for granted, but Jesus spoke to people who knew total darkness in a way that we do not. He uses the image of light again and again to describe his ministry and presence: 'I am the light of the world. Whoever follows me will never walk in darkness but will have the light of life' (John 8:12). He also uses it to describe the ministry of his disciples, who received the light from him: 'You are the light of the world. A city built on a hill cannot be hidden' (Matthew 5:14).

It is in this sense that Jesus speaks here, inviting his followers to consider carefully their response to his light. Is what you think to be light actually darkness? Do you need to turn again to God and let him illuminate your life? One thing is for sure, when we invite Jesus to be our light, he dispels all darkness and shines vividly within us so that our lives shine with the same illumination that we see in him.

Quoting the story of creation, where the first thing God creates is light, Paul puts it brilliantly when he writes, 'For it is the God who said, "Let light shine out of darkness", who has shone in our hearts to give the full light of the knowledge of the glory of God in the face of Jesus Christ' (2 Corinthians 4:6).

Prayer

Lord Jesus, shine on me. Illuminate my life and shine through me.
Let your light in me illuminate the world.

STEPHEN COTTRELL

Doing the right thing

While [Jesus] was speaking, a Pharisee invited him to dine with him; so he went in and took his place at the table. The Pharisee was amazed to see that he did not first wash before dinner. Then the Lord said to him, 'Now you Pharisees clean the outside of the cup and of the dish, but inside you are full of greed and wicked-ness. You fools! Did not the one who made the outside make the inside also? So give for alms those things that are within; and see, everything will be clean for you.'

Now we get down to some of the nitty-gritty application of this wisdom. The Jewish people had all sorts of laws and ritual customs that shaped everyday life and helped create their identity as a people. The Pharisees are shocked when they see Jesus ignoring them. That does not mean Jesus thinks the law is unimportant, but he does react strongly against the fastidious application of complicated rituals when the heart of the law is ignored. Taking great care to wash the outside of a cup when your inner being is corrupted by greed and wickedness is not the way of God. Clean yourself first, is the message of Jesus.

We may live in a far more relaxed sort of society when it comes to the rituals that shape everyday life (indeed, it would be quite good if we got some of them back!), but what matters is the inner motivation. An inner cleanliness of motive and desire is the gift of God's grace and forgiveness, refining our minds and wills so that our everyday actions, however small, will be done in service to God and to others. This way of approaching life is sometimes called 'practising the presence of God'—that is, living every moment as if in the very presence of God and, therefore, offering every thought and action to God. It is the fruit-ful outworking of Christian wisdom and the sign that Christian faith has become Christian life.

Prayer

Wise and loving God, help me to know your presence with me every day. May my actions serve your glory and work for the building of your kingdom in the world.

STEPHEN COTTRELL

Facing conflict

[Jesus said] 'And I tell you, everyone who acknowledges me before others, the Son of Man also will acknowledge before the angels of God; but whoever denies me before others will be denied before the angels of God. And everyone who speaks a word against the Son of Man will be forgiven; but whoever blasphemes against the Holy Spirit will not be forgiven. When they bring you before the synagogues, the rulers, and the authorities, do not worry about how you are to defend yourselves or what you are to say; for the Holy Spirit will teach you at that very hour what you ought to say.'

Following in the way of Jesus leads to conflict. The world is very good at rejecting wisdom, especially wisdom that challenges the innate self-centredness of the human heart.

Towards the end of Luke 12 (v. 49), Jesus says, 'I came to bring fire to the earth', and, in Matthew's Gospel (10:34), 'Do not think that I have come to bring peace to the earth; I have not come to bring peace, but a sword'. These are hard sayings. They do not contradict the central truths of the Christian faith that, as Paul says (Colossians 1:20), through Christ, 'God was pleased to reconcile to himself all things', but we are living though the birth pangs of this new reality. Consequently, we will find ourselves in conflict with those earthly powers and principalities that are always bent on the destruction of what is good. After all, Jesus himself was beaten and crucified and he asks us to carry a cross (Luke 9:23). Hence, in our passage today, Jesus does not say '*if*' they bring you before the authorities (v. 11), but '*when*'. There is a sober acknowledgment that following Jesus will mean difficulty, but there is also comfort: 'The Holy Spirit will teach you at that very hour what you ought to say'. Notice, however, that this wisdom is not delivered in advance: it is when the hour comes that the Holy Spirit will be at hand. Just trusting God's provision when and where we need it is wisdom that we could all usefully learn.

Prayer

Holy Spirit, teach me to trust in your provision.

STEPHEN COTTRELL

Treasure in heaven

Then [Jesus] told them a parable: 'The land of a rich man produced abundantly. And he thought to himself, "What should I do,
for I have no place to store my crops?" Then he said, "I will do
this: I will pull down my barns and build larger ones, and there I
will store all my grain and my goods. And I will say to my soul,
'Soul, you have ample goods laid up for many years; relax, eat,
drink, be merry.'" But God said to him, "You fool! This very night
your life is being demanded of you. And the things you have prepared, whose will they be?" So it is with those who store up
treasures for themselves but are not rich towards God.'

Now here is a story. We have looked quite a bit at the subject of wisdom
in Luke's Gospel, but only had one story. This is unusual because Jesus
is the great storyteller, so much of his wisdom is given in stories, not
statements. Also, Luke's Gospel is, arguably, the Gospel with the greatest stories in it! This, in turn, reveals an important truth about truth: it
cannot be pinned down.

The truth about Jesus is the truth about a person and it is learned
through a relationship. That is why the stories themselves are puzzling
and challenging. They are either like this one—very obvious and therefore very disturbing—or else enigmatic and perplexing so that you need
to keep coming back to them to find out more.

Here is a man enjoying all the riches and rewards that life has to
offer. Without a care in the world, he can plan ahead with confidence
and suck the marrow of a very comfortable life. It is at this very
moment, though, with his future secure, that he dies. The heart of life
lies in seeking the presence and the purposes of God in each moment,
so that we store up lasting treasure and learn to sit lightly to the so-
called treasures of the world.

Prayer

Generous God, reveal your presence in each moment of my life,
that I may store up treasure in heaven.

Stephen Cottrell

LUKE 12:22–31 (NRSV, ABRIDGED)

Seek first the kingdom

[Jesus] said to his disciples, 'Therefore I tell you, do not worry about your life, what you will eat, or about your body, what you will wear... Consider the ravens: they neither sow nor reap, they have neither storehouse nor barn, and yet God feeds them. Of how much more value are you than the birds! And can any of you by worrying add a single hour to your span of life?... Consider the lilies, how they grow: they neither toil nor spin; yet I tell you, even Solomon in all his glory was not clothed like one of these. But if God so clothes the grass of the field... how much more will he clothe you—you of little faith! And do not keep striving for what you are to eat and what you are to drink, and do not keep worrying. For it is the nations of the world that strive after all these things, and your Father knows that you need them. Instead, strive for his kingdom, and these things will be given to you as well.'

In the light of this wisdom—that we can dwell in God's presence and find there our security and affirmation—we come now to this important passage where Jesus, pointing to God's created order, shows how it, too, reveals God's wisdom and provision. As the psalmist puts it (Psalm 19:1), 'The heavens are telling the glory of God; and the firmament proclaims his handiwork'.

The ravens do not sow. They do not even own barns—like the rich man's in yesterday's story, who looked for security in his own wealth—but they are still fed. The lilies, too, do not spin, but they are still wonderfully clothed. Likewise, we do not need to strive for food or security: 'Give us our daily bread' is the only prayer that we need. Instead, we must seek God's kingdom—'your will be done'—and then everything else will be added.

What is this kingdom? Well, it is not measured by boundaries of time or space. It is about living under the rule of God—that just and gentle rule inaugurated in Christ.

Prayer
Lord Jesus, show us your kingdom.

STEPHEN COTTRELL

A new heart

'Do not be afraid, little flock, for it is your Father's good pleasure
to give you the kingdom. Sell your possessions, and give alms.
Make purses for yourselves that do not wear out, an unfailing
treasure in heaven, where no thief comes near and no moth
destroys. For where your treasure is, there your heart will be also.'

When Jesus was born, wise men came to visit him, symbolising the
wealth and wisdom of the world bending the knee before what God was
doing in Jesus Christ. Wise people still find their way to Christ and
those who wish to be wise sit at his feet. When we do this, he gives us
his kingdom. We are not just citizens of this kingdom but also, with
Christ, co-heirs (Romans 8:17).

The values of this kingdom seem odd to the world. They demand a
new set of relationships—not just with God and with each other but
also with the planet itself and all the possessions that we have hitherto
considered so important. We must not only sit lightly to the things of
the world but also walk lightly on the surface of the earth. First, because
it is not ours to do with as we wish and, second, because our true home
is with Christ himself. This is the unfailing treasure of heaven. It
requires a purse that will not wear out, one that no burglar can pinch.
Such a purse is made of those attitudes and values that we see lived so
abundantly in Christ, which we now seek, by the working of the Holy
Spirit, to inculcate in ourselves. Above all, it involves an open heart,
ready to receive from God. As Proverbs puts it, 'Keep your heart with all
vigilance, for from it flows the springs of life' (4:23).

We need not fear. More than anything else, that is what God wants
to give us—a new heart. It is the Father's good pleasure to draw us into
new and loving relationships and for us to draw from him the kindly
wisdom that changes the world.

Prayer

Bountiful God, give me a new heart and lead me to the wisdom of Christ.

STEPHEN COTTRELL

The last shall be first

'Be dressed for action and have your lamps lit; be like those who are waiting for their master to return from the wedding banquet, so that they may open the door for him as soon as he comes and knocks. Blessed are those slaves whom the master finds alert when he comes; truly I tell you, he will fasten his belt and have them sit down to eat, and he will come and serve them. If he comes during the middle of the night, or near dawn, and finds them so, blessed are those slaves.'

We finish where we started, with a story about someone being served at table. We are told that we must be like faithful servants who are waiting for the master's return, who are ready to serve him as soon as he comes knocking at the door. We are to be both Martha and Mary, attentive to Jesus and ready to serve him. Then there is a twist—one so subtle that I expect many people have read this little story many times and not even noticed it. The master returns; the servants are ready, dressed for action, with their lamps lit. In the upside-down economy of the kingdom of God, however, the tables are turned. The master returns all right, but, instead of sitting down and receiving their service, *he waits on them*! It is an astonishing turnaround: the master becomes an attentive Mary and a bustling Martha. He fastens his belt, sits the servants down and serves *them*.

Who but a God who eats with sinners, washes feet and welcomes strangers could tell such a story? God serves us in the kingdom where the first are last and the humble lifted high. Like the Lord's mother, let us treasure this wisdom in our hearts (Luke 2:51) and live it all our days.

Prayer

*Merciful God, I thank you for the service you have shown me in Christ,
and for the wisdom you put in my heart. Help me to serve Christ in others,
to be attentive to his word, to look for his coming,
and to live as a child of his kingdom.*

STEPHEN COTTRELL

Don't forget to renew your annual subscription to *New Daylight*! If you enjoy the notes, why not also consider giving a gift subscription to a friend or member of your family?

You will find a subscription order form on pages 155 and 156. *New Daylight* is also available from your local Christian bookshop.

Pilgrimage through Holy Week and Easter

During the next two weeks, I invite you to accompany me on a pilgrimage to some of the places that are closely associated with Jesus' final days on earth and some of his resurrection experiences.

I am often asked, when I lead pilgrimages, what the precise legacy of the various sacred places is. For me, there are two main legacies. First, there are those people connected to the individual places, who have drawn out their significant sacredness. I believe it is that sacredness which continues to draw others to these places. Second, that sacredness, which pilgrims seek and often discover, helps them to make some crucial connections in their own lives. Pilgrimage helps us to identify those particular and personal times and experiences when the deep journey of the heart and the physical journey of life connect or coincide. This is what we mean when we say that pilgrimage is about both an inner and an outer journey—and, when the connection is made, we are able to bring together some of the significant key moments in our lives and our experience of God's creative and redeeming love.

So, the challenge facing the pilgrim at the beginning of each journey is this: 'Am I open enough to be a pilgrim? Am I courageous enough to live with some of the risks and uncertainties that go with pilgrimage?' Unlike a package holiday to the sun, a pilgrimage cannot be tidily arranged and neatly compartmentalised. There will be exploration, discovery, complex questions and a whole variety of personal encounters... but that is life, too, is it not?

'I was glad when they said to me, "Let us go to the house of the Lord!" Our feet are standing within your gates, O Jerusalem. Jerusalem—built as a city that is bound firmly together. To it the tribes go up, the tribes of the Lord, as was decreed for Israel, to give thanks to the name of the Lord... Pray for the peace of Jerusalem' (Psalm 122:1–4, 6).

Note that the Bible passages printed in the following notes are sometimes shorter than the references given. Try to make time to read the longer passage if you can.

Andrew Jones

Weeping on the Mount of Olives

As [Jesus] came near and saw the city, he wept over it, saying, 'If you, even you, had only recognised on this day the things that make for peace! But now they are hidden from your eyes.'

I have often walked from the old city of Jerusalem into the Kidron Valley, up through the Garden of Gethsemane, then to the eastern edge of the Mount of Olives. The view from the top is breathtaking!

About half way up the Mount of Olives stands a church called Dominus Flevit ('the Lord wept'), which commemorates Jesus weeping over Jerusalem. Interestingly, it is built in the shape of a tear. In the east window is the image of a chalice and, beyond the window, you can see the old city, as if the whole city is being reflected out of the chalice. It is the city that Jesus wept over, and the chalice recalls God's will for Jesus.

As we pause in this valley, let us remember that Jesus' tears were not ones of fear or selfishness, but, rather, tears for those who had rejected his message of love. Throughout his ministry, Jesus' overriding call was for people to repent of their sins and turn their hearts towards God, but they refused. For me, as I sat in Dominus Flevit, it was the very heart of Jesus that came to mind. Jesus wept here in compassion and love for his people. He continues to weep with people today as they refuse to heed the message of God's kingdom. Today, the tear-filled heart of Jesus is still wide open to receive each one of us. It is there that we will find comfort and deliverance in the midst of so many sufferings.

This place not only reveals the eternal love of Jesus but also marks the spot where that final 'drama' of God's redeeming love turned decisively towards the cross, the ultimate symbol of love.

Reflection

On this Palm Sunday, we are invited to follow Jesus—to stay close to his love and also suffer his tears. As we make the commitment to follow him, we will be rewarded as inheritors of the kingdom of God.

ANDREW JONES

Cleansing the temple

Then [Jesus] entered the temple and began to drive out those who were selling things there; and he said, 'It is written, "My house shall be a house of prayer"; but you have made it a den of robbers.'

One of the most fascinating views from the Mount of Olives is the old temple site, which today is dominated by the golden dome of the Al-Aqsa mosque. This place is considered sacred by Jews, Muslims and Christians alike. It is where Abraham prepared his son Isaac as a sacrifice to witness his utter faithfulness to God. It is the site of the ancient temples of David, Solomon and Herod, where the ark of the covenant was once protected. It is where Jesus, as a young boy, instructed the teachers and where he was to return many times with his family as a pilgrim.

Nowadays, the site belongs to the Muslims and the mosque has been built around the rock from which Muhammad rose to heaven. Over many hundreds of years, people have quarrelled and fought for this place. Even today, Orthodox Jews believe that the site is so holy that nobody should be allowed even to walk on it. As entry to the site is forbidden to Jews, they venerate the place from outside the Western Wall (once called the Wailing Wall), as it still contains the massive stones of Herod's second temple.

Today, as we continue our pilgrimage through Jesus' final few days, we pause to remember his entry into the temple, disrupting the stalls of the moneymakers and declaring it to be a house of prayer. It is a pivotal moment in Holy Week: it is an almost desperate attempt to make clear the core of Jesus' message and underlines the central place of prayer and spirituality for those who seek to follow him. Throughout his ministry, Jesus was clear that it is purity of life and prayer that lie closest to the heart of our faith as Christians. That must be the thrust of our proclamation today.

Prayer

Help us, Lord, to respect each other despite our differences. You, Lord, are the true and eternal temple and in you we find our dwelling.

ANDREW JONES

Teaching with authority in the temple

Every day [Jesus] was teaching in the temple. The chief priests, the scribes, and the leaders of the people kept looking for a way to kill him; but they did not find anything they could do, for all the people were spellbound by what they heard.

Pilgrimage is a very ancient practice and a devotion that connects a great many people of different faiths, traditions and cultures. For that reason alone, we should consider its contemporary appeal. Over the generations, Jews have traditionally made pilgrimages to Jerusalem, Muslims to Mecca, Buddhists to the Himalayas, Hindus to the Ganges and we Christians have constructed a network of special places where we believe there has been some kind of divine presence at some stage.

As a religious person living in a time saturated with religious activity, Jesus must have accompanied his family on pilgrimages. We know from the Gospels that pilgrimage was a popular devotional activity. According to Luke's Gospel, Jesus told the parable of the good Samaritan on his way from Galilee to Jerusalem with his disciples, so, possibly, he was on one such pilgrimage to the holy city.

Today we pause to remember his teaching in the temple during that first 'Holy Week'. So often with pilgrims, I have stopped in sacred places to read a Bible passage and consider its relevance for today. Doing this at some of the places Jesus once visited is of particular importance, but it can be difficult—maybe even a little dangerous—to generalise about the significance of Jesus' teaching for our contemporary situations. Of course his teaching is central to our faith and vital for Christian living. At the same time it is unique in the sense that it contains a fresh message that appeals to each of us as distinct and very different individuals. We all have a unique relationship with Jesus and Holy Week is the ideal time to renew and refresh that relationship, to see what lessons he would have us learn today.

Reflection

As we consider Jesus' teaching ministry towards the end of his life, may we, like the people in and around the temple, be spellbound by what we read and the sense we each make of it.

ANDREW JONES

Resting awhile in Bethany

Six days before the Passover Jesus came to Bethany, the home of Lazarus, whom he had raised from the dead. There they gave a dinner for him. Martha served, and Lazarus was one of those at the table with him.

Some years ago, I walked from Bethany to Jerusalem in an attempt to immerse myself in the experience and commotion of Jesus' final few days. We know from the Gospels that he had close friends in Bethany, including Mary, Martha and Lazarus. What struck me about my visit to Bethany was how many of the churches in the vicinity contained various symbols of love—indeed 'love' was a kind of Bethany theme. During that concluding week in his earthly life, Jesus encountered much opposition, persecution and pain, but, in Bethany, in the company of his friends, he encountered love and friendship. There, Jesus' friends welcomed him, loved him and made room in their hearts for him.

Today there stands a modern Catholic church, run by the Franciscans, over what was once the home of Mary, Martha and Lazarus. Near the entrance there are some interesting words on a plaque, which seek to convey this 'Bethany theme': 'Today as in the past, the love of Jesus seeks a refuge where he is lovingly expected and where he can rest. He finds our hearts are filled with distractions—people, work, our own interests. He longs for us to empty our hearts and lovingly receive him'.

Before we come to the last three days before Jesus' death, let us pause awhile in Bethany to remind ourselves that, in his love, Jesus still seeks a 'Bethany' in our midst—hearts that will offer him a welcome. Of course, we also know from scripture that when we serve each other, we serve Christ. Similarly, from Christian teaching down the centuries, we know that the way in which we best recognise Jesus today is to see him in each other. So, by seeking a 'Bethany' in our midst, Jesus calls us to be a Bethany for each other and for strangers.

Reflection

Let your heart be a Bethany for me and for me and for me and for me…

ANDREW JONES

Pondering the future in Gethsemane

Then Jesus went with them to a place called Gethsemane; and he said to his disciples, 'Sit here while I go over there and pray'... Then he came to the disciples and said to them, "Are you still sleeping and taking your rest? See, the hour is at hand.'

St Mark's Church in Jerusalem stands over the place traditionally associated with the last supper. At the time when Jesus hosted that meal, Jews would have been busy preparing for their Passover celebrations. For them, as for Jesus, it was a time to remember God rescuing his people from captivity in Egypt and making a covenant with them. Jewish people all over the world continue to do precisely that to this day.

Over that supper, Jesus made a new covenant (*mandatum novuum*, hence the name 'Maundy', from the Latin for 'commandment')—this time, a covenant between God and all his 'children' everywhere, not exclusively those in 'Egypt'. As we celebrate the last supper on this holy day, we remember with Jewish people everywhere that first covenant and God's liberating power, but we also sing of the new covenant, remembering this time the way in which the Old Testament prophecies are fulfilled in Christ.

Just before I left St Mark's Church on one occasion with a group of friends, we sang the *Hallel* (words from the group of Psalms 113—119), as Jesus and his group would have done at the end of the last supper. As we left, we crossed the Kidron Valley again and entered the garden of Gethsemane. It is there that Jesus lingered on the night before he died, along with his disciples, and where he pondered his destiny and prayed. From his prayer, Jesus emerged with renewed confidence that strengthened him to face what lay ahead.

As we pause on this Maundy Thursday, let us follow Jesus' example in Gethsemane and receive anew the power of faith so that we can give ourselves confidently to the service of Christ and others.

Prayer

Lord, remember that we are weak and always ready to avoid suffering. We pray that you will give us the faith you gave to Jesus so that we may face our own crosses with courage.

ANDREW JONES

Suffering on the hill of Calvary

Then they brought Jesus to the place called Golgotha (which means the place of a skull). And they offered him wine mixed with myrrh; but he did not take it. And they crucified him.

Every pilgrimage to Jerusalem inevitably includes the traditional Way of the Cross (Via Dolorosa) at some point. The custom of following this Via Dolorosa and offering prayers, hymns and readings at each of the 14 stations of the cross, commemorating various episodes in Jesus' final journey, has been important to many Christians since at least the 15th century. The first nine stations are located in churches and streets in the old city while the final five are housed within the Church of the Resurrection (sometimes called the Church of the Holy Sepulchre). Each of the traditional Christian denominations—including the Eastern ones—has a chapel here. Sunday mornings are very lively and noisy as they all worship at about the same time!

On one occasion in the Church of the Resurrection, I remember climbing up the steps on to what is regarded as the site of Calvary, the twelfth station. Located deep within the church, here were the remains of an old quarry that once stood outside the city walls. Then I moved to the 13th station to behold the depiction of a dead Jesus lying in the arms of his mother. That station is a simple altar on which are the words *Stabat Mater*, recalling (in Latin) Mary standing by the cross—a far cry indeed from scenes we can imagine of her earlier life, as a proud mother enjoying better times in Nazareth. Yet, we know that both these elements are crucial for a holistic Christianity. That is, both the cradle and the cross are essential partners in our faith—a faith rooted deeply in the birth, death and resurrection of Christ; a faith rooted deeply in our own birth, death and resurrection.

Reflection

From a wall plaque in the Church of the Resurrection: 'We can only give Jesus thanks for his redemption when we choose to follow his path of love—a love that does not shirk suffering but sacrifices itself and even prays for its enemies.'

ANDREW JONES

Burying Jesus as a family

Then Joseph bought a linen cloth, and taking down the body, wrapped it in the linen cloth, and laid it in a tomb that had been hewn out of the rock. He then rolled a stone against the door of the tomb. Mary Magdalene and Mary the mother of Joses saw where the body was laid.

The final station of the Via Dolorosa is the site within the Church of the Resurrection traditionally associated with the empty tomb. Today's structure is an attempt to reconstruct the tomb rediscovered in AD326 by the Emperor Constantine's architects in a nearby hillside. There is another site outside the city walls called the garden tomb and some Christians think that is the more accurate site. It certainly gives a good impression of what the site may well have looked like 2000 years ago. I encourage pilgrims to go to both places.

Whichever place we prefer, it is where we move from a deep sense of hopelessness and tragedy to one of great hope and joy. We are all familiar with the story of how the women went to the grave early that Sunday morning and found it empty. It is hard to get our heads round what exactly happened on that most powerful of mornings, but there is no doubt the disciples believed wholeheartedly that Christ had been resurrected. Without their faith and their witness there would be no talk of Jesus, no Gospel written and certainly no Church.

Augustine once said in a sermon on the empty tomb that, as Christians, we are an Easter People and Alleluia is our song. Precisely because Jesus conquered death, the earliest Christians set out to chronicle the accounts concerning his life, but the story continues in each one of us. As we end our journey along the Via Dolorosa and leave the Church of the Resurrection, we carry with us those same stories that the first Christians were so keen to share.

Reflection

Some words on a plaque near one of the chapels of the Church of the Resurrection: 'Jesus is searching for people to humble themselves as he did. Will you be that disciple today?'

ANDREW JONES

JOHN 20:1–10

Discovering an empty tomb

Early on the first day of the week, while it was still dark, Mary Magdalene came to the tomb and saw that the stone had been removed from the tomb... Then the other disciple, who reached the tomb first, also went in, and he saw and believed.

I have already mentioned that pilgrimage is something that all major world religions do. For many non-Christians, part of their religious heritage is a particular bit of land and to overlook the emphasis they place on that land is to overlook one of their most persistent and passionately held doctrines. Jewish people, for instance, would regard Israel and especially Jerusalem as central to their relationship with God. Any threat to this idea of centrality and the relationship stemming from it can lead to chaos and disorder. Jerusalem is held by Jews (as Mecca is to Muslims) to be the place where God has given an abundance of material gifts to his chosen people. They feel a real and intimate connection with the land of Israel, which builds cohesion, patriotism, union and kinship.

The New Testament does not avoid such passionately held convictions, but it also transcends the basic concept of spiritual place. Easter Day shows us that we find holy space wherever the risen Christ is. The thrust of the Easter experience is that, as Christians, we personalise holy space in the Resurrection of Jesus Christ. For the true holiness of place, the Christian tradition has fundamentally substituted the holiness of the person of Jesus Christ.

Encountering the risen Christ on that first Easter Day brought a new truth of his presence into the lives of his disciples then, as it does now. Although 'finished', he was found anew in a garden, in a room, on a beach, on a road. Although 'gone', he is present anew in hearts and communities. He is remembered anew in his church today as we continue to proclaim his eternal presence and abiding love.

Reflection

We sing today that Christ is alive and living with us. We sing today that Christ is fulfilled and completed. We sing today of Christ our heartbeat and our rebirth.

ANDREW JONES

Appearances in the garden

Mary stood weeping outside the tomb... Jesus said to her 'Mary!'
She turned and said to him in Hebrew, 'Rabbouni' (which means
Teacher)... Mary Magdalene went and announced to the disciples,
'I have seen the Lord'... Jesus came and stood among them and
said, 'Peace be with you.'

The drama of Holy Week comes to its climax in the resurrection of
Christ. During this Easter week, we now need to sit back and ponder all
that we saw and heard and prayerfully begin to ask what it means to us.

The resurrection appearances in the garden reveal two important
truths. The first is the role of the women, including Mary Magdalene,
who came to the tomb early. They were courageous in remaining at the
crucifixion. They stood in solidarity with the shamed figure of their
Lord while others shouted words of abuse. They were generous and
respectful in coming to anoint his dead body. As we reflect on this, the
resurrection can raise us to live beyond ourselves, too.

The second is the greeting of 'peace be with you'. In Welsh, there are
two words for 'peace'—*heddwch* and *tangnefedd*. The first is used more
or less as 'peace' is used in English: 'We pray for the peace of the
world', for instance. The second has a deeper and more spiritual meaning and is equivalent to the phrase that the risen Christ shares with his
disciples. It is interesting that, at almost all the resurrection appearances, Jesus shares his peace before he does anything else. It is the
peace that will bind us to God and bind us together as a Christian
community.

As we reflect on the meaning of Easter for us 21st-century disciples,
as the risen Christ bids us that same greeting of peace, how do we hear
it? So often, within our hearts, God's own dwelling place in us, there is
tribulation and sadness and a deep need for peace.

Reflection

Let us pray today for hearts that abound with Christ's true peace—
tangnefedd. *It is in this way that the new Jerusalem will be built:*
a community of disciples anxious to promote tangnefedd
at every given opportunity.

ANDREW JONES

Returning to the upper room

A week later his disciples were again in the house, and Thomas was with them. Although the doors were shut, Jesus came and stood among them and said, 'Peace be with you.'... Thomas answered him, 'My Lord and my God!'

We cannot say with certainty where the disciples stayed in the days immediately after the resurrection—the text simply refers to a 'house' or a 'room'—but I tend to think it could well have been the same room where the last supper was shared, the upper room. The Gospels record at least two occasions when the disciples gathered in that room and, on both occasions, the risen Christ greeted them and gave them the gift of his peace.

Pilgrims to Jerusalem are still shown what could well have been the location of the upper room, known today as the Cenacle. According to Epiphanius (a fourth-century bishop of Salamis and a native of Jerusalem), a small Christian church existed on the site of the room from the time of Hadrian (AD117–38). Epiphanius suggests that it was possibly the only church in Jerusalem until after the conversion of Constantine. Interestingly, Acts 1:13 states that it is also where the disciples stayed during Pentecost.

Jesus' second resurrection appearance in that room was to Thomas. All four evangelists identify Thomas as one of the Twelve and John refers to him as the one who doubted the resurrection until encountering the risen Christ, when he confessed his faith overwhelmingly.

Our journey along the Via Dolorosa last week was coloured by suffering and sadness, but, today, the picture is completely fresh and hopeful and Thomas' confident response to Jesus is so reassuring. It is the stuff of true witness to a living God and, in our busy, mad world, pausing with Thomas is a timely reminder that we continue to celebrate both the resurrection itself and our own contemporary experience of it.

Prayer
Lord God, in you we trust. Help us when we face doubts about our faith. Bless us with your gift of reassurance so that we may be confident witnesses of your presence today.

ANDREW JONES

Walking together towards Emmaus

Now on that same day two of [the disciples] were going to a village called Emmaus, about seven miles from Jerusalem... When [Jesus] was at table with them, he took bread, blessed and broke it, and gave it to them.

Let us walk together towards Emmaus. Like so many of the places associated with the life of Jesus, we cannot be certain of the location and there are actually four possibilities. The first is a place called Imwas—first recognised as Emmaus by Eusebius and Jerome around the fourth and fifth centuries AD. This site has always been of strategic significance as it controls the major routes from the coast to Jerusalem. For me, this is the Emmaus of reconciliation because of the work there today of the Trappist monks, the Jesus-Bruderschaft community and the Neve Shalom, seeking to bring different people and traditions together.

The second site, Abu Gosh, was chosen by the Crusaders in the twelfth century. For me, it is the Emmaus of beauty because of the peace and serenity surrounding the church there and the Benedictine community and their gardens. The third site, Qubeilah, is a town on another main route from Jerusalem to the coast, which pilgrims began to use after the period of the Crusaders. For me, this is the Emmaus of liturgy because of the great annual gathering of the Latin Church there on Easter Monday. It has been strongly suggested that Motza, the name of the fourth site, is derived from Emmaus and referred to as Ammous by the first-century historian Josephus. For me, it is the Emmaus of desolation because the Arab village of Qulunia on this spot was violently destroyed in 1948.

Pilgrims can visit all four sites as each brings to mind one of the four hallmarks of the journey to Emmaus. Reconciliation—the disciples were reconciled to Christ; beauty—this resurrection experience is perhaps the most beautiful of all; liturgy—the disciples recognised Jesus through a liturgical action, the breaking of bread; desolation—we continue to live in a marred world and are challenged to bring into it the resurrection peace.

Prayer

Lord, may Emmaus be a living encounter for us.

ANDREW JONES

Sharing breakfast by the lake

Just after daybreak, Jesus stood on the beach... Jesus said to them, 'Come and have breakfast.' Now none of the disciples dared to ask him, 'Who are you?' because they knew it was the Lord.

Our pilgrimage moves north, to Galilee, to a place called Tabgha on the lake where Jesus is remembered for feeding the 5000 (Matthew 14:13–21) and appearing to his disciples on the beach after the resurrection. There he showed that those who believe in his word and remain faithful to his teaching will experience kingdom gifts.

The disciples had clearly returned to their families and were back at work. This particular morning they were struggling to catch any fish, but, on obeying Jesus and casting their nets in a different direction, they made a remarkable catch. The risen Christ asked them to do something completely contrary to the norm—to cast their nets in daylight! The large haul of fish was not a direct result of the disciples' skills but faithful obedience to Christ's word, even if it meant taking a risk or approaching the situation from a brand new perspective.

There have been a number of theories about the number of fish caught—153—but the one I favour links the number to Aristotle, the Greek philosopher who taught in Athens about 400 years before the birth of Christ. One of his passions was nature and he managed to identify 153 different species of fish! John may well have been familiar with some of Aristotle's work and, thus, keen to compare the net to the emerging Christian community, with the believers as the fish. If so, then there is room for all the fish of the world in the net, as there is room for all the different types and groups of people in the Church.

Sometimes it is not easy to make sense of what Christ is asking of us, because it may not please us or suit us. Through obedience to his word, though, and responding positively to his invitations—even if they are risky and, at times, uncomfortable—we come to recognise that we are doing God's will.

Prayer

Give us grace, Lord, to hear your word and, on hearing it,
respond with joy and confidence.

ANDREW JONES

ACTS 1:6–11

Bidding farewell... for now!

When [Jesus] had said this, as they were watching, he was lifted up, and a cloud took him out of their sight... Two men in white robes stood by them. They said, '... This Jesus, who has been taken up from you into heaven, will come in the same way as you saw him go into heaven.'

Today we come to the Church of the Ascension, commonly known as the Eleona Grotto. Once again, we descend into the Kidron Valley and travel up the Mount of Olives, quite close to where we began our pilgrimage a fortnight ago. It is good to bring our pilgrimage to a close here because, although we have travelled together to commemorate some of the key moments in the final part of Jesus' earthly life and resurrection, we need to consider how it all affects us.

Before his departure, Christ promised that he would send us the Holy Spirit as a continuing presence, to remain among us, and he himself would return again. This two-fold promise has deep consequences for us. It calls us to never tire of being prepared to greet Christ either as he comes to us through and in others or when he physically comes again. It also challenges us to live in the knowledge that we already have one foot in the kingdom. The whole of Jesus' life—his teaching, suffering, death and resurrection—was about inaugurating the kingdom of God.

It has never been part of the Christian tradition to believe that the kingdom is something entirely in the future. Rather, it is already in our midst and the way we live and the way we are must always seek to reflect its values that Christ shared with us. Of course, the completion of the kingdom still lies in the future and that is what we pause to ponder here as we gaze upwards, as the disciples once did, and remember Christ's ascension promises.

Reflection

Some words on a plaque close to the Eleona Grotto: 'When the trumpet call sounds at midnight, only those whose hearts are tuned to the sound will hear it. They are a people who love Jesus and who wait expectantly for him.'

ANDREW JONES

Reflecting on the journey home

Then [the disciples] returned to Jerusalem from the mount called Olivet... When they had entered the city, they went to the room upstairs where they were staying... All [of them] were constantly devoting themselves to prayer, together with certain women.

There are always four parts to any pilgrimage: the preparation, journey, destination and homecoming. Today, we come to the fourth part and, as the disciples returned to Jerusalem in the power of the Holy Spirit, so we return home, renewed and refreshed by what we have seen, heard and shared.

Returning home from somewhere special, having shared some powerful things, can often be a time of mixed emotions. There may be the sadness of bidding farewell to people we have grown close to, the excitement of having had some amazing experiences and the joy of returning home and telling the stories. In this sense, a pilgrimage never has a clear and definite ending. Rather, it is a living and eternal experience that can develop and blossom as each of us grows more and more in faith.

This Holy Week and Easter pilgrimage has shown us that a true witness of faith is rooted in a living experience of the risen Christ in our own daily concerns. A pilgrimage is as much an inner journey as that which we do on our feet, and is not ultimately dependent on outward circumstances: they simply help our journey to progress. In other words, any effective pilgrimage is a reflection of our whole lives. With each step we take at the sacred places visited, we have the opportunity to reflect on where we have been in our lives, where we are now and how best we may move forward, to make those significant connections. Our pilgrimage throughout our lives is a journey of the heart that started in God and will end in God. As Christians, we have been assured that Jesus Christ is the way to God, the truth about God and the life in which we discover God.

Reflection

Thou art the journey and the journey's end.

Boethius, Roman philosopher (fifth–sixth century AD).

ANDREW JONES

The God of Jacob

I find it amazing, and also deeply encouraging, that God should choose to identify himself by the names of his followers, weak and fallible as they are. In the Bible, he introduces himself as the God of Abraham, Isaac and Jacob and he does so without apology or embarrassment (Exodus 3:6, 15–16; Matthew 22:32; Acts 3:13).

These three men were, of course, the Old Testament patriarchs, the fathers of the nation of Israel, and it was to them that the covenant promises were given. Their lives were lived by faith and they followed God's lead as best they could. Yet, each of them was flawed and it is only through grace that they are honoured in this way.

Of the three, it is the inclusion of Jacob that is most surprising as even a quick glance at his story shows that he was something of a scoundrel and a rogue and the least 'worthy' of honour. To confound our sense of merit even more, we find that God is often identified specifically with this conman, being called the God of Jacob, the Mighty One of Jacob, and even the Holy One of Jacob (Psalm 46:7, 11; 132:2, 5; Isaiah 29:23).

Perhaps the main principle behind the story of Jacob is just this: that God chooses to use whoever he wants, and that he works on the basis of grace rather than human merit, of undeserved favour, not well-earned reward.

What the story of Jacob also shows—and this will be the focus of the passages that follow—is that God can take the most unlikely of people and shape and fashion them into instruments fit for his purpose. Jacob's story is, above all, a story of transformation. When God takes hold of our lives, he does so for a purpose: to make us like his Son and use us for his glory. We are blessed in order to become a blessing (Genesis 12:2–3), which is God's agenda for us all.

There is something of the Jacob in each of us, but here is the encouragement: if God could make something out of his unpromising life, he can make something out of ours!

Tony Horsfall

GENESIS 25:21–26 (NIV, ABRIDGED)

Sibling rivalry

Isaac prayed to the Lord on behalf of his wife, because she was childless. The Lord answered his prayer, and his wife Rebekah became pregnant. The babies jostled each other within her, and she said, 'Why is this happening to me?'... When the time came for her to give birth, there were twin boys in her womb. The first to come out was red, and his whole body was like a hairy garment; so they named him Esau. After this, his brother came out, with his hand grasping Esau's heel; so he was named Jacob.

Jacob and Esau were born in answer to Isaac's prayer and after 20 years of waiting. Only the childless understand the pain of not having children. Likewise, only those with children can understand the pain that they can bring—not just at birth but also throughout their lives.

The turmoil inside Rebekah's womb was a foreshadowing of the rivalry there would be between the two boys in their lives and the strife that would come to the family through them. They were twins, but in no way alike. Different in appearance and temperament, they were rivals from the start—a rivalry that would be passed on to their descendants.

Jacob in particular seems to have had a grasping nature. He was named Jacob because it means 'he deceives' or 'he supplants', and his grasping of his brother's heel illustrates the ambition and striving for pre-eminence that would characterise him for much of his life. Jacob typifies the strong, independent self that wants to get ahead in life, by whatever means, and without God.

The Bible calls this independent self 'the flesh' (Romans 8:5–8; Galatians 5:19–21) and it is present in each of us, but shows itself in different ways. If we are to be used by God, we need to become aware of how 'the sinful nature' operates in our own lives and work with God to overcome its influence. The story of Jacob shows how God works in the life of an individual to bring about that transformation.

Prayer
Make me aware, Lord, of my own unhelpful ways, and help me to change.

TONY HORSFALL

The birthright

The boys grew up, and Esau became a skilful hunter, a man of the open country, while Jacob was content to stay at home among the tents. Isaac, who had a taste for wild game, loved Esau, but Rebekah loved Jacob. Once when Jacob was cooking some stew, Esau came in from the open country, famished. He said to Jacob, 'Quick, let me have some of that red stew! I'm famished!'... Jacob replied, 'First sell me your birthright.' 'Look, I am about to die,' Esau said. 'What good is the birthright to me?'

The years pass by and the rivalry between the two boys is managed, but never actually dealt with; it simmers away under the surface. This may be a family already in the stream of God's purpose, but it is a dysfunctional one, disfigured by parental favouritism and marred by sibling rivalry. Tension is rising and an explosion is inevitable.

Jacob is prone to deceit, full of ambition, and resents being the second son. The quieter of the two, he must have brooded for many years on the injustice of being the younger by only minutes. His eye is on the birthright that belongs to his brother, which would guarantee a larger share of the family inheritance.

When Esau returns famished from a day in the countryside, Jacob sees his opportunity and drives a hard bargain: a bowl of soup (traditionally described as a 'mess of pottage') for the rights of the firstborn son. Here we see selfish ambition in action, the grasping for position and power that is also so destructive of relationships in churches and Christian organisations (James 3:14–16; 4:1–2).

What of Esau? An outdoor extravert, he has no time for reflection; he is too busy enjoying life. Here is a man who is a prisoner of his bodily appetites, what scripture calls the 'lust of his eyes' (1 John 2:16), and for whom immediate gratification is all that matters. Higher values are sacrificed for the pleasures of the moment, which is a tragic way to live and always brings regret (Hebrews 12:16–17), yet how many make the same mistake?

Prayer

Awaken me, Lord, to any sinful tendency in my own life.

Tony Horsfall

GENESIS 27:5–10 (NIV, ABRIDGED)

The blessing

When Esau left... to hunt game and bring it back, Rebekah said to her son Jacob, 'Look, I overheard your father say to your brother Esau, "Bring me some game and prepare me some tasty food to eat, so that I may give you my blessing..." Now, my son, listen carefully and do what I tell you: go out to the flock and bring me two choice young goats, so I can prepare some tasty food for your father... Then take it to your father to eat, so that he may give you his blessing before he dies.'

The strife within the family is set to escalate even further as the time comes for Isaac to die. Already physically weak and almost blind, the old man has one final and important duty to perform—transferring the family blessing to his eldest son. It is far from an empty ritual, for the blessing is the blessing of God and the one receiving it will become the channel of the covenantal promises given by God to Abraham.

Perhaps we can read this episode as indicating that Esau inherited from Isaac his love of good food and impulsive nature. Rebekah has passed on to her favoured boy (Jacob) her ability to scheme and plot. Here, we observe how she sees a way for Jacob to receive the coveted blessing. Thus, mother and son conspire together to deceive the father and cheat the older brother. The initiative comes from Rebekah, but Jacob is happily complicit and his ability to tell a barefaced lie hoodwinks his unsuspecting and gullible father. Their elaborate scam is a success and, dressed as his brother and pretending to be Esau, Jacob receives the blessing.

Needless to say, Esau is furious when he discovers what has happened (v. 38), but the nature of the blessing is that, once given, it cannot be revoked. Murderous thoughts enter Esau's heart and a deep-seated grudge lodges within him (v. 41). The family is now divided. Jacob has won his prize, but it will cost him dearly.

Prayer

Lord, help me to be honest in all my ways.

TONY HORSFALL

GENESIS 27:41–44 (NIV, ABRIDGED)

Exile and estrangement

Esau held a grudge against Jacob because of the blessing his father had given him. He said to himself, 'The days of mourning for my father are near; then I will kill my brother Jacob.' When Rebekah was told... she sent for her younger son Jacob and said to him, 'Your brother Esau is planning to avenge himself by killing you. Now then, my son, do what I say: Flee at once to my brother Laban in Harran. Stay with him for a while until your brother's fury subsides.'

Resentment is one of the most destructive emotions we experience as human beings. It is anger turned inwards and can be expressed in the form of a grudge—a settled disposition of hostility towards another person arising out of a specific incident. There is always a reason for a grudge: we feel we have been mistreated in some way and so we feel justified in maintaining our hostile stance, even allowing it to intensify with time. This we call 'nursing' a grudge.

No one would be surprised by Esau's response to Jacob's deceitfulness, for he was badly wronged, but holding a grudge robs us of our joy and inner peace so we lose twice over. The two brothers are now estranged and it will be many years before they are reconciled. How easily friendships are spoilt and family ties broken by a lack of forgiveness!

Jacob, for his part, is forced to run away from home like a coward, with the guilt of what he has done as his only companion. Conscience is a God-given faculty to help us know right from wrong and it condemns us when we fail to act according to what we know to be true. We can only surmise that Jacob's conscience is still operative and that he regrets his behaviour. He, too, will have some long and lonely years in which to mull over his actions.

Rather than bring the brothers together, Rebekah's solution is to drive them further apart by sending Jacob back to Haran and the ancestral home, a backward step in every sense.

Prayer

Lord, help me to deal wisely with my anger and cherish my relationships.

TONY HORSFALL

I dreamed a dream

[Jacob] had a dream in which he saw a stairway resting on the earth, with its top reaching to heaven... There above it stood the Lord, and he said: 'I am the Lord, the God of your father Abraham and the God of Isaac. I will give you and your descendants the land on which you are lying. Your descendants will be like the dust of the earth... All peoples on earth will be blessed through you and your offspring. I am with you and will watch over you... and I will bring you back to this land. I will not leave you until I have done what I have promised you.'

Leaving home with nothing but what he can carry, a chastened Jacob sets off for Haran, alone and dejected. He is learning the hard way that 'a man reaps what he sows' (Galatians 6:7) and the discipline of God is at work in his life, whether he realises it or not.

With only a stone for a pillow, Jacob lays his head down. Night has fallen in more than one way and darkness engulfs his soul. God, however, is a God of grace and his grace is greater than all our sin. God speaks to Jacob through a dream, confirming that the promises made to Abraham are now to be worked out through him. No one could be more undeserving of such favour than Jacob, no one more deserving of disfavour, but the nature of grace is that God gives us what we do not deserve. The purpose of God to bless all people will continue despite the unworthiness of those who carry the promises.

Grace is not fair. It does not add up logically and, in that sense, it is scandalous. It is totally undeserved, which is what the story of Jacob is meant to convey, but, notice this: while grace is free, it is not cheap (as Bonhoeffer famously said). Jacob is now the one through whom God will work and that means he will come even more under the discipline of God so that the divine purposes are accomplished.

Reflection
God can draw a straight line even with a crooked stick.

TONY HORSFALL

116

GENESIS 28:16–22 (NIV, ABRIDGED)

The blind made to see

When Jacob awoke from his sleep, he thought, 'Surely the Lord is in this place, and I was not aware of it.' He was afraid and said, 'How awesome is this place! This is none other than the house of God; this is the gate of heaven.' … He called that place Bethel… Then Jacob made a vow, saying, 'If God will be with me and will watch over me on this journey… then the Lord will be my God and this stone that I have set up as a pillar will be God's house.'

Jacobs's encounter with God at Bethel represents the start of spiritual awakening in his soul. Bethel means 'house of God' and, for possibly the first time in his life, Jacob becomes aware of the divine presence. Until this moment, he had lived in spiritual darkness, despite his ancestry, but now the light has been turned on.

Jacob would have heard the stories of faith regarding his grandfather Abraham, but they had probably meant little to him. What faith he had may have been simply second-hand and without relevance to his own life. He had been blind to God's presence and deaf to his voice. How easy it is to live surrounded by the things of God and yet not know him personally!

Jacob's awakened soul is overwhelmed by fear, but fear of a good kind—what the Bible calls the 'fear of the Lord'. It is that humble regard for God birthed in us when we realise how great he is and how small we are.

Jacob's response is a mixture of faith and self-interest. He makes a vow (vv. 20–22), which is not quite a prayer but, rather, a negotiation with God about the future. He believes now, but still assumes that he is in control. The bargain is that if God looks after him, the Lord can be his God and he will even give him (such generosity!) a tenth of his wealth.

Jacob has much to learn, but at least his faith journey has truly begun. Like all of us, he will need to be released from self-centredness if he is to be a blessing to others.

Prayer

Lord, make me aware of your presence today.

TONY HORSFALL

The rough made smooth

After Jacob had stayed with him for a whole month, Laban said to him, 'Just because you are a relative of mine, should you work for me for nothing? Tell me what your wages should be.' Now Laban had two daughters; the name of the older was Leah, and the name of the younger was Rachel. Leah had weak eyes, but Rachel had a lovely figure and was beautiful. Jacob was in love with Rachel and said, 'I'll work for you seven years in return for your younger daughter Rachel.'

Jacob arrives at Haran with the hand of God firmly on his shoulder. This unlikely object of God's choice is to be shaped into an instrument fit for the master's use. God will use a mixture of crisis (as at Bethel and, later, Peniel) to break his pride, and process (long years of hardship in exile) to soften his character. The rough will be made smooth, but it will take time. As we watch God at work in his life, we see a pattern for how he works in each of us.

God often uses hard circumstances and difficult people to knock off our rough edges. In Haran, God works through Laban—a devious man even more ruthless than Jacob who has no scruples in cheating his young nephew. Jacob receives a taste of his own medicine and learns what it feels like to be swindled. Aware of Jacob's love for the beautiful Rachel, Laban takes advantage of him and tricks him into marrying the less attractive Leah. Instead of working seven years for his bride, Jacob finds himself toiling another seven years before Rachel can be his (vv. 22–30).

None of us enjoys being trained by God because it is often painful, but God disciplines us in love and for our good, so that we can share his holiness (Hebrews 12:4–11). The fact that God is at work in our lives, shaping and forming us, is a mark of God's acceptance of us and a reminder that he has a purpose for us. Often we fight against what he is doing rather than accept the positive correction he brings.

Reflection

How is God changing you?

TONY HORSFALL

God is not in a hurry

[Jacob said to Laban] 'I have been with you for twenty years now... This was my situation: the heat consumed me in the daytime and the cold at night, and sleep fled from my eyes. It was like this for the twenty years I was in your household. I worked for you fourteen years for your two daughters and six years for your flocks, and you changed my wages ten times. If the God of my father... had not been with me, you would surely have sent me away empty-handed. But God has seen my hardship and the toil of my hands.'

Twenty years is a long time—perhaps a quarter of someone's life. For Jacob, they may have felt like wasted years, hidden away in the back-water of Paddan-Aram, tending sheep. For a homesick young man, it must have seemed like an eternity, but God is never in a hurry and soul-shaping work cannot be rushed.

In reality, much was happening during those hidden years. Hardship was doing its work, producing in Jacob resilience and strength of character. Time spent alone gave him the chance to reflect on his ways and consider the past. Laban's rough treatment humbled him, making him more compassionate towards others. All the while, he became more aware of God's presence and able to recognise his goodness towards him.

Those years were also years of blessing. Everything he did seems to have prospered and, despite Laban's persistent opposition, Jacob increases in wealth, having his own flocks and servants (30:30, 43). During this time, too, eleven children are born to him—the beginning of the fulfilment of God's promise that his descendants would be numerous (28:14). So, there is much happiness in his life as well. God not only uses hardship to soften us but also, sometimes, his kindness is what draws us to him (Romans 2:4).

Eventually, Jacob feels the time has come to return to his homeland (Genesis 30:25–26), but, again, Laban resists him. Timing is everything with God and it is another six years before God speaks to him the word that will release him from exile (31:3).

Prayer
Lord, my times are in your hand.

TONY HORSFALL

The prayer of a humble heart

Then Jacob prayed, 'O God of my father Abraham, God of my father Isaac…. who said to me, "Go back to your country and your relatives, and I will make you prosper," I am unworthy of all the kindness and faithfulness you have shown your servant. I had only my staff when I crossed this Jordan, but now I have become two camps. Save me, I pray, from the hand of my brother Esau, for I am afraid… But you have said, "I will surely make you prosper and will make your descendants like the sand of the sea."'

Eventually the time comes for Jacob to return home and confront his past. He knows that he will have to meet Esau and is deeply afraid, assuming that Esau will seek revenge. It takes courage to face up to our mistakes and put right things that are wrong, but Jacob's time in Haran has made him ready to take such a brave initiative.

Jacob's prayer reflects the depth of his relationship with God now and is so different in tone from the vow he made at Bethel. Notice four things in particular. First, he moves in response to God. It is not because he has predetermined what he will do, but because God has told him the time has come to return. Doing his own will has given way to doing God's will. Second, he recognises how much he owes God and does not take any credit for his success. He knows that he is unworthy of blessing and that everything is from God. Glorifying self has given way to glorifying God. Third, he realises his need of God and humbly asks for help, rather than hiding his fear. Self-sufficiency has given way to God-dependency. Finally, he trusts in the promise of God and believes that what God has said to him will come to pass. Self-confidence has given way to God-confidence.

What a long way Jacob has come in his spiritual journey! There is more work to be done, however, and the gentle process of the last 20 years will presently give way to the violent crisis at Jabbok.

Prayer
Lord, how I thank you for changing me.

TONY HORSFALL

GENESIS 32:22–26 (NIV, ABRIDGED)

The strong made weak

That night Jacob... took his two wives, his two female servants and his eleven sons and crossed the... Jabbok. After he had sent them across... he sent over all his possessions. So Jacob was left alone, and a man wrestled with him till daybreak. When the man saw that he could not overpower him, he touched the socket of Jacob's hip so that his hip was wrenched as he wrestled with the man. Then the man said, 'Let me go, for it is daybreak.' But Jacob replied, 'I will not let you go unless you bless me.'

Jacob has been preparing to meet Esau, but it is God he encounters first. Having said goodbye to his family and his servants and detached himself from his possessions, Jacob is left again empty-handed and alone. It is the perfect setting for a life-changing encounter and Jacob appears to be intuitively aware that something will happen.

Bible scholars generally regard this as a 'theophany'—recognising in a stranger an appearance of God. It is certainly a mysterious incident and the unprovoked attack on Jacob must have taken him by surprise. He responds as he normally would, summoning all his natural strength to protect himself, wrestling with his opponent throughout the night. It shows what a tough character he was.

In the morning, the divine wrestler realises that Jacob will not easily surrender, so taps him on the hip to weaken him. It is a wound of love and now, defeated and disabled, Jacob seems to realise the true identity of his opponent. Refusing to let him go, Jacob clings to the stranger in desperation, seeking his blessing: 'I will not let you go, unless you bless me' (v. 26). Jacob knows that what he needs most is the blessing of God, the tangible confirmation that God is with him. Is that not the greatest need of each of us and our churches? Without that divine dimension to what we do, our labour may well be in vain (Psalm 127:1). God is not reluctant to bless, but often we are not determined enough in our asking.

Prayer

Lord, I stand in need of your blessing, just as Jacob did.

TONY HORSFALL

The rascal made royal

The man asked him, 'What is your name?' 'Jacob,' he answered. Then the man said, 'Your name will no longer be Jacob, but Israel, because you have struggled with God and with humans and have overcome.' Jacob said, 'Please tell me your name.' But he replied, 'Why do you ask my name?' Then he blessed him there. So Jacob called the place Peniel, saying, 'It is because I saw God face to face, and yet my life was spared.' The sun rose above him as he passed Peniel, and he was limping because of his hip.

The work of transformation God has been doing in Jacob's life is now acknowledged in the giving of a new name. He is no longer the person he was, and he and others are to be made aware that he has become a different person.

In Old Testament times, your name was indicative of your character, so the disclosure of Jacob's name (meaning 'deceiver') represents an acknowledgment by him of who he was and how he had behaved. Self-awareness—and the removal of all self-deception—is a vital step on the way to transformation. The meaning of his new name (Israel) is some-what uncertain, but some suggest 'one who rules with God' and, there-fore, 'prince'. It is meant to convey a new relationship with God and a new spiritual status of intimacy and favour. This change in standing has occurred because Jacob has come through the struggles in his life (with both people and circumstance) and emerged as a better person, having allowed God to transform him. He was defeated in his struggle with the stranger, but was victorious in his struggle with himself. Brokenness becomes the way to blessing.

The stranger refuses to disclose his own identity. Perhaps Jacob's ques-tion indicates our human desire to understand God and label him, but the stranger's refusal is a reminder of the mystery of God, who is ulti-mately unknowable. Any knowledge we have of him is, at best, partial (1 Corinthians 13:12). Peniel marks a new place of fellowship with God for Jacob. He is not only blessed but also able now to be a blessing.

Prayer

Lord, may I know you more deeply.

TONY HORSFALL

Big boys do cry

Jacob looked up and there was Esau, coming with his four hundred men; so he divided the children among Leah, Rachel and the two female servants. He put the female servants and their children in front, Leah and her children next, and Rachel and Joseph in the rear. He himself went on ahead and bowed down to the ground seven times as he approached his brother. But Esau ran to meet Jacob and embraced him; he threw his arms around his neck and kissed him. And they wept.

If estrangement was the theme of Jacob's early life, reconciliation is the theme now. He knows that he must make his peace with Esau, but fears the worst, afraid for himself and his family. God, however, has been working in the lives of both men and the time is ripe for them to be reunited.

The Bible has much to say about forgiveness and reconciliation (Matthew 5:24; Colossians 3:13–14), but we all know it is not easy in practice. Once relationships have been broken, it is hard to restore trust. Even when the pain has subsided, it is not always possible to put things back together again. Only the intervention of God can begin to make it possible.

What is clear in this wonderful story is that, over the years since they parted, God has been at work in both men and they are not the same. Jacob we know about, because we have his story before us, and his humble attitude and genuine sorrow make it easier for his brother to forgive him. The proud, self-seeking deceiver is no more.

The change in Esau is equally amazing. We do not know how God has worked in him, but his willingness to forgive his double-deceiving twin shows evidence of a deep work of grace. All thought of revenge and getting equal have vanished. He longs to find his brother again. In traditional British culture, men do not weep easily, so I find it deeply moving to imagine the scene here as they embrace.

Reflection

Perhaps today's scene is a good one to keep in mind as we think about those with whom we may need to be reconciled.

TONY HORSFALL

GENESIS 35:9–15 (NIV, ABRIDGED)

Welcome home

After Jacob returned... God appeared to him again and blessed him. God said to him, 'Your name is Jacob, but you will no longer be called Jacob; your name will be Israel.'... And God said to him, 'I am God Almighty; be fruitful and increase in number...' Then God went up from him at the place where he had talked with him. Jacob set up a stone pillar at the place where God had talked with him, and he poured out a drink offering on it... Jacob called the place where God had talked with him Bethel.

Having lived overseas for a time, I know what a wonderful feeling it is to arrive home again, to familiar surroundings and people. Jacob has longed to return for many years and now, finally, he is back in Canaan and the place where he first encountered God, Bethel. 'Coming home' is a wonderful metaphor to describe our relationship with God and the sense of acceptance, welcome and love we experience when we are restored to fellowship with him. It is what we were made for and where we belong.

Home is where we are known for who we really are. As Jacob returns, he is reminded of his new identity as Israel, a prince with God. It is easy to forget who we are in God and to take our identity from what we used to be or how other people see us. It takes spiritual discipline to shape our identity from who we are now, based on what God says about us. Even then, we have to grow into our new identity and become who we really are. That takes time and patience.

Home is also where we can share freely and this period of Jacob's life is characterised by communion with God. Three times in this chapter we are told that God talked with him, which suggests conversation, a dialogue rather than a monologue. There is a developing intimacy between Jacob and God now and a natural flow of communication.

Bethel means 'house of God' and God's purpose is that we should feel at home with him.

Prayer

Lord, thank you that you welcome us with open arms.

TONY HORSFALL

Blessing others

Then [Jacob] blessed Joseph and said, 'May the God before whom my fathers Abraham and Isaac walked faithfully, the God who has been my shepherd all my life to this day, the Angel who has delivered me from all harm—may he bless these boys. May they be called by my name and the names of my fathers Abraham and Isaac, and may they increase greatly on the earth.'

We have not been able here to cover every aspect of Jacob's life, but our final passage illustrates how deep the work of transforming grace has gone. The one who has been such a grasper, thinking only of himself, has now become the one who loves to give and is able to bless others.

We can already see the wider purposes of God for Jacob being fulfilled. Jacob's twelve sons will be the basis of the nation of Israel, as each will become a tribe. By the time they go down to join Joseph in Egypt, they already number 70 people (Genesis 46:26–27). The great saving act of God in calling out a people for himself to bless all nations is well under way.

Two things are natural for Jacob to do as he nears the end of his life. The first is to acknowledge the work of God, how he has been divinely guided and protected. Long before David penned his famous psalm, Jacob could say 'The Lord is my shepherd.' The second is to pray for God's blessing on his grandchildren, that they may know God personally and be part of his ongoing purpose in the world.

God's intention for each of us is that we know his blessing and become a blessing to others. This starts with our own families, but extends far beyond our own circle to any we meet who are in need. We begin within our own communities and cultures, but then develop a concern beyond even that so we have a worldwide focus. Blessing is never intended to be kept for oneself, but to be given away in ever-widening circles.

Prayer
Lord, show me how I can be a blessing to others.

TONY HORSFALL

Proverbs 30 and 31

Over the next ten days, we shall be looking at the last two chapters of the book of Proverbs. Proverbs is a work full of Israel's traditional wisdom—a literary gathering of teaching that would have been passed down from parents to children and teachers to students within Israel's centuries-old oral tradition.

Despite the apparent accessibility of much of the teaching, the work still presents us with something of an enigma. In the words of Raymond C. Van Leeuwen, 'We often find ourselves listening in on a fragmentary conversation intended for someone else and filled with hidden assumptions and references' ('The Book of Proverbs' in *The New Interpreter's Bible*, Volume V, p. 19). Dating the work has proved difficult as it was compiled over several centuries and, in the entire book, the only specific historical references to people we know are those to Solomon (1:1, 10:1) and Hezekiah (25:1). Those named at the beginning of our two chapters, Lemuel and Agur, are otherwise unknown.

Another difficulty for some is posed by the ancient patriarchal worldview of the original text. Some of our modern translations tend to shield us from this reality, translating as 'my child' or 'children' the Hebrew words for 'son' or 'sons' (compare the NIV's 'son' and the NRSV's 'child'). Yet, there is a balance: women *are* to be found within the text and are not only mentioned negatively or simply in terms of their relations with men. Wisdom, for instance, is personified as a woman (8:1, 9:1) and there are numerous references to the fact that father and mother together were responsible for their children's upbringing and education (1:8; 6:20; 17:25; 19:26).

The main challenge when approaching any ancient text would appear to be twofold. First, we need to allow the words to speak across time with their own internal integrity—to respect the worldviews of the cultures that gave them birth and allow any dissonance that arises when held alongside our own lives and experience to stand. Second, we need to seek the wisdom of the God of *every* age, whose living word transcends the specific emphases of different cultures and civilisations, circumstances and times, including our own.

Barbara Mosse

Living with unanswered questions

The words of Agur son of Jakeh. An oracle. Thus says the man: I am weary, O God, I am weary, O God. How can I prevail? Surely I am too stupid to be human; I do not have human understanding. I have not learned wisdom, nor have I knowledge of the holy ones. Who has ascended to heaven and come down? Who has gathered the wind in the hollow of the hand? Who has wrapped up the waters in a garment? Who has established all the ends of the earth?... Surely you know!

How easy do we find it to live with unanswered questions? The speaker in today's passage—Agur?—proclaims his weariness to God: he has not 'learned wisdom' (v. 3) and berates himself for being 'too stupid to be human' (v. 2). He hurls the 'big questions' at God, appealing to and for the divine wisdom he feels that he lacks.

There is an interesting parallel here with the closing chapters of the book of Job. There, the same questions are asked, complete with the statement, 'Surely you know!' (Job 38:5). The twist there is that it is *God* who is asking these questions, challenging Job's presumption (Job 38—39). The way to wisdom for Job lies not in greater and greater knowledge but acceptance and the worship of the God of awe and mystery whose ways are not our ways (Isaiah 55:8–9).

There is some resonance also between today's passage and the world-weary pessimism of the 'Teacher'—the writer of Ecclesiastes—for whom 'all is vanity and a chasing after wind' (Ecclesiastes 1:14). The Teacher, however, is at least one step ahead of Agur on the road to true wisdom. Agur seems to believe that the acquiring of more wisdom will give him definitive answers to his questions, while the Teacher already knows that knowledge can only take human beings so far (Ecclesiastes 1:16–18). Beyond that, we have to 'step out into the darkness and put [our] hand into the hand of God' (Minnie Louise Haskins, 1908).

Prayer and reflection

'But I trust in you, O Lord; I say, "You are my God." My times are in your hand...' (Psalm 31:14–15).

BARBARA MOSSE

The food that I need

Two things I ask of you; do not deny them to me before I die: remove far from me falsehood and lying; give me neither poverty nor riches; feed me with the food that I need, or I shall be full, and deny you, and say, 'Who is the Lord?' or I shall be poor, and steal, and profane the name of my God.

At the beginning of 2 Chronicles (1:7–12), God appears to the newly crowned King Solomon and asks him what gifts he would like to be granted. Solomon asks not for wealth, honour or long life but 'wisdom and knowledge to go out and come in before this people, for who can rule this great people of yours?'

The words of Agur we consider today stem from a like sense of humility and awareness of human frailty. These few verses constitute the only prayer in Proverbs, and the two requests—to be guarded from falsehood and lying and a plea that the speaker may know neither wealth nor poverty—seem at first to be unrelated. Yet, there is a link. In Hosea 4:1–2 God's indictment of the people of Israel include 'stealing' and 'lying' among the actions that indicate the nation's faithlessness. Agur is fully aware that the path of falsehood is a slippery slope, leading imperceptibly from the seemingly innocuous 'white lie' to a deeper and graver disloyalty.

The second request is familiar to us in its more positive form: 'Give us this day our daily bread' (Matthew 6:11). Agur asks for enough to live, but neither so much that he becomes complacent and forgetful of God's mercies, nor so little that he is tempted to dishonour God and distrust his provision by stealing from others. All the dimensions of this prayer are therefore concerned with certain aspects of behaviour and outlook having the potential to damage human relationships and bring dishonour to God—dishonesty, greed, complacency and envy— together with the personal insight and request for divine wisdom needed for their avoidance.

Prayer and reflection

'Our Father in heaven, hallowed be your name… Give us this day our daily bread… And do not bring us to the time of trial' (Matthew 6:9, 11, 13).

BARBARA MOSSE

Honour your parents

There are those who curse their fathers and do not bless their mothers... The eye that mocks a father and scorns to obey a mother will be pecked out by the ravens of the valley and eaten by the vultures.

The fifth commandment offers a positive consequence to the honouring of one's parents—long life 'in the land that the Lord your God is giving you' (Exodus 20:12). Our passage today from Proverbs 30, however, gives the shadow side of this commandment: 'The eye that mocks a father and scorns to obey a mother will be pecked out by the ravens of the valley and eaten by the vultures' (v. 17). The image of the eye here resonates sharply with the law of retribution, which fits the punishment to the crime—that is, 'eye for eye, tooth for tooth', Leviticus 24:20, underlining the teaching that cursing one's parents is utterly wrong. The teaching continues, subtly, in the New Testament. For example, when the twelve-year-old Jesus is finally discovered debating with the religious leaders in the temple by his distraught parents, 'he went down with them and came to Nazareth, and was obedient to them' (Luke 2:51).

There is more to this than simply the rightness of treating your parents respectfully. When Paul writes to his young disciple Timothy (2 Timothy 1:5), he comments on Timothy's sincere faith: 'a faith that lived first in your grandmother Lois and your mother Eunice and now, I am sure, lives in you'. Ancient cultures tended to treat their parents and elders with a natural respect—a tendency still evident among tribal peoples today. Elders held the tribal memory and, consequently, were treated with great honour and reverence. They were seen as both the repositories of knowledge and wisdom and the transmitters of those qualities to the young. When we reflect on aspects of our society today, it is perhaps difficult to avoid an awareness of what we have lost.

Prayer and reflection

Lord, help us to respect and learn from the wisdom of those who have gone before us... What signs can we see, in our own families and in society as a whole, of our respect for or neglect of 'the wisdom of the elders'?

BARBARA MOSSE

How can these things be?

Three things are too wonderful for me; four I do not understand:
the way of an eagle in the sky, the way of a snake on a rock, the
way of a ship on the high seas, and the way of a man with a girl.
This is the way of an adulteress: she eats, and wipes her mouth,
and says, 'I have done no wrong.'

Numerical sayings were common in the ancient world, and verses
18–19 offer a three-plus-four example that is alive with poetic resonance. In this passage, the pattern has no literal meaning, but is used
to underline the writer's simple wonder at a number of marvellous
phenomena in the created world. He marvels at the inbuilt wisdom of
the eagle and the snake, which seem to know instinctively the way God
created them to be, and he is in awe of the skill that enables the sailor
to navigate his ship with safety in dangerous and unfathomable waters.
The pinnacle of his wonder is reached with the miracle and mystery of
sexual love and the realisation that all these marvels of God's creation
are beyond human comprehension.

This is not the garden of Eden, however, and verse 20 indicates how
easily the sacred quality of God's creative gifts can be abused. The application of the term 'way' to each character in these verses indicates a
poetic rendering of a familiar teaching: the idea of the 'two ways'—of
the righteous and of the wicked—which is fundamental to the worldview and spiritual outlook of both Proverbs and the Psalms (Psalm 1
and 37; Proverbs 10–15). The choice of images in these verses is deliberate, too, depicting the three realms of creation (air represented by the
eagle, earth by the snake and water by the ship). The narrative then
moves to the human realm. Humanity is seen as the crown of God's
creation, but with that honour comes the privilege and responsibility of
choice—whether opting for good or for ill.

Reflection

'This God—his way is perfect… For who is God except the Lord? And who
is a rock besides our God?—the God who girded me with strength, and
made my way safe' (Psalm 18:30, 31).

BARBARA MOSSE

Weakness and wisdom

Four things on earth are small, yet they are exceedingly wise: the ants are a people without strength, yet they provide their food in the summer; the badgers are a people without power, yet they make their homes in the rocks; the locusts have no king, yet all of them march in rank; the lizard can be grasped in the hand, yet it is found in king's palaces.

Only the number four appears in this passage, as the writer refocuses his attention on the world of nature as a source of wisdom and right living. This is not a new idea: in Job 12:7–10, the animals, birds and plants are declared to be the teachers of humanity and, for the psalmist, 'the heavens are telling the glory of God; and the firmament proclaims his handiwork' (Psalm 19:1).

In today's passage, the innate, God-given wisdom of the creatures is emphasised and much is made of the paradox that then arises from their smallness, weakness and insignificance. The ants may be 'a people without strength' (v. 25), but that does not prevent them from providing adequate food for themselves and their children. The badgers are 'a people without power' (v. 26), but they are well able to make homes. At other points in the book of Proverbs, the provision of food and the building or care of a house are seen as fundamental indications of wisdom (9:1; 14:1; 27:27; 31:15). The locusts in our passage today have no leader, 'yet all of them march in rank' (v. 27). The main source of wisdom here seems to lie in their unity and the strength of their social organisation.

Jesus taught that a type of wisdom is to be found in children, whom society generally believed should be seen and not heard (Matthew 18:3–4), and a similar sentiment finds a voice earlier in Old Testament teaching (Psalm 8:2). In our own lives and relationships and daily experiences, where do we look to find wisdom? Do we allow ourselves to be surprised by where we may find it?

Prayer and reflection

'Truly I tell you, unless you change and become like children, you will never enter the kingdom of heaven' (Matthew 18:3).

BARBARA MOSSE

Cause and effect

Under three things the earth trembles; under four it cannot bear up: a slave when he becomes king, and a fool when glutted with food; an unloved woman when she gets a husband, and a maid when she succeeds her mistress… If you have been foolish, exalting yourself, or if you have been devising evil, put your hand on your mouth. For as pressing milk produces curds, and pressing the nose produces blood, so pressing anger produces strife.

The two short extracts that form today's passage act as the 'sandwich' surrounding the 'filling' of yesterday's extract. In the first part, we are given another three-plus-four numerical saying, all of which represent, to some degree, an upending of what was perceived to be the natural order of things. Such patterns of inversion were not unusual in the ancient world and could fulfil a variety of functions—some serious, some comedic—with yet others offering a combination of the two. The coming of God's Messiah was believed to have been indicated by an upending of the natural order. In the words of Hannah (1 Samuel 2:4–8) and Mary (Luke 1:51–53), those of low status would be raised up and the powerful and mighty humbled.

There is more to be appreciated in today's passage than merely the writer's wit and humour, however. The particular images chosen reflect the ancient idea that the natural world is inextricably linked to the world of human behaviour and relationships. Chaos in the human realm will inevitably correlate with disharmony in the natural world ('the earth trembles'). In Celtic Christian tradition, the idea of the human person as an integral part of the entirety of God's creation, whose behaviour inevitably affects the whole, is paramount.

Does the idea of a correlation between the natural world and human behaviour still hold true today? If so, in what areas may we be experiencing its effects, both positively and negatively?

Reflection

'The whole creation has been groaning in labour pains until now; and… we ourselves, who have the first fruits of the Spirit, groan inwardly while we wait for adoption, the redemption of our bodies' (Romans 8:22–23).

BARBARA MOSSE

Wise kingship

The words of King Lemuel. An oracle that his mother taught him: No, my son! No, son of my womb! No, son of my vows! Do not give your strength to women, your ways to those who destroy kings. It is not for kings, O Lemuel, it is not for kings to drink wine, or for rulers to desire strong drink; or else they will drink and forget what has been decreed, and will pervert the rights of all the afflicted… Speak out for those who cannot speak, for the rights of all the destitute. Speak out, judge righteously, defend the rights of the poor and needy.

The narrative now moves on from the words of Agur to those of King Lemuel—although those first words are simply a reporting of advice given to him by his mother.

What impassioned advice it is, though: 'No, my son! No, son of my womb! No, son of my vows! Do not give your strength to women, your ways to those who destroy kings' (vv. 2–3). Although no names or dates are given, it is difficult to read these words and not be reminded of the fate of Samson—one of Israel's judges in the pre-monarchy period. Samson was a famous sexual incontinent whose downfall ultimately came about as a result of 'giving his strength'—and, naively, his trust—to the treacherous Delilah (Judges 13—16).

In this matter and in the temptations of drink, Lemuel's mother is clearly aware of the dangers. A king should not be adding to the suffering of the afflicted, but should speak out for them and defend their rights with justice and compassion. The underlying concern here, however, is not simply with the issues themselves but also the fact that intemperate behaviour adversely affects the ability of the person to discern wisely and act appropriately. Lemuel is being urged to choose his friends wisely and discern his future path with care. We do not have to be kings to appropriate such wisdom for ourselves.

Reflection

'Make me to know your ways, O Lord; teach me your paths… Who are they that fear the Lord? He will teach them the way that they should choose' (Psalm 25:4–5, 12).

BARBARA MOSSE

A capable wife

A capable wife who can find? She is far more precious than jewels. The heart of her husband trusts in her... She does him good, and not harm, all the days of her life. She seeks wool and flax, and works with willing hands... She rises while it is still night and provides food for her household and tasks for her servant-girls... She is not afraid for her household when it snows, for all her household are clothed in crimson... She makes linen garments and sells them; she supplies the merchant with sashes... Her children rise up and call her happy; her husband, too, and he praises her: 'Many women have done excellently, but you surpass them all.'

It is not clear whether today's passage forms an integral part of the 'oracle' of King Lemuel's mother or has been inserted into the narrative from another source. Either way, the 'capable wife' described here is, without doubt, the kind of woman Lemuel *should* be seeking—one who will enhance his reputation and encourage his strengths with her own.

Over time, there have been varied reactions to this passage. Some feminists have rejected it, seeing it as one of many examples of the Bible keeping women in their place; others have dismissed it as an impossible ideal. Both such reactions miss the point, however. The verses comprise a hymn to wisdom where 'a woman who fears the Lord' (v. 30) and her accomplishments act as a counterpart to 'the man who fears the Lord' (NIV 1984) of Psalm 112. The two passages are acrostics (where each line begins with successive letters of the Hebrew alphabet) and both focus on the wise and energetic activity of the person described.

The aim here, then, is not to paint a picture of some unattainable ideal but to highlight the underlying values of wisdom and discernment under God that enable a person to live rightly, justly and to the full measure of their God-given ability. Whoever we are and whatever responsibilities we have in life, these values remain as necessary and vital today as ever.

Reflection

'You desire truth in the inward being; therefore teach me wisdom in my secret heart' (Psalm 51:6).

BARBARA MOSSE

PROVERBS 31:16–18, 21, 25

A capable *wife?*

She considers a field and buys it; with the fruit of her hands she plants a vineyard. She girds herself with strength, and makes her arms strong. She perceives that her merchandise is profitable... She is not afraid for her household when its snows, for all her household are clothed in crimson... Strength and dignity are her clothing, and she laughs at the time to come.

A close reading of Proverbs 31 poses challenges to those who may be tempted to cite it as biblical support for the idea that a woman's place is solely in the home, caring for her husband and children. If that was intended to be the message, then the verses chosen for today's passage read a little strangely. Verse 16 tells us, 'She considers a field and buys it' and one commentary at least is sufficiently embarrassed by this statement to say that it must mean something different, because Israelite women could not own land (*The New Interpreter's Bible*, Vol. V, p. 261).

The descriptive language used here deepens the enigma: 'She girds herself with strength, and makes her arms strong... Strength and dignity are her clothing...' (vv. 17, 25). This language has a distinctly masculine flavour. Indeed, elsewhere it is God who girds the warrior with strength for the battle (Psalm 18:39) and God is described as 'girded with might' (Psalm 65:6). So, while, on the one hand, the passage is busy extolling the virtues of perfect womanhood, on the other it is quietly subverting itself and discouraging us from lapsing into complacent stereotypes.

'Dignity' is the overriding quality with which this wisdom is associated, and accompanies the living of 'a quiet and peaceable life in all godliness' (1 Timothy 2:2). The strength and dignity of our 'capable wife' is such that she is able 'laugh at the time to come' (Proverbs 31:25)—not out of any lack of care or responsibility, but because of sensible provision against future need (v. 21).

Reflection

How easy do we find it in today's world to strike a healthy balance between attending to the needs of the present moment and making sensible (rather than neurotic) provision for the future?

BARBARA MOSSE

PROVERBS 31:26, 28, 30–31

The fear of the Lord

She opens her mouth with wisdom, and the teaching of kindness is on her tongue... Her children rise up and call her happy; her husband too, and he praises her... Charm is deceitful, and beauty is vain, but a woman who fears the Lord is to be praised. Give her a share in the fruit of her hands, and let her works praise her in the city gates.

So it is that this ancient wisdom hymn comes to its triumphant conclusion: the woman speaks with kindness and wisdom, and her husband and children praise her. That wisdom of speech and action is seen not as a natural human attribute but as one that arises from fear of the Lord (v. 30).

The reference to the 'city gates' (v. 31) is intriguing. In each town, the leading citizens (the 'elders') would come each day to the gate. Here the community's affairs would be discussed (Genesis 23:10; Job 29:7) and matters of law would be assessed and resolved (Amos 5:12, 15; Zechariah 8:16). The gate was also the place where commercial dealings were transacted—including the buying and selling of fields (Proverbs 31:16). The city gates were normally a male preserve, but it would seem that the woman depicted here had some part in the business dealings that went on there. She is actively involved and it is therefore right that she be given 'a share in the fruit of her hands' (v. 31).

Ultimately, however, neither this hymn nor its acrostic twin, Psalm 112, are concerned with particular male or female behaviour. We saw earlier that, at various points in this chapter, vocabulary more usually associated with the masculine has been used. In a similar way, 'the man who fears the Lord' of Psalm 112 (NIV 1984) displays 'feminine' as well as 'masculine' qualities ('gracious and compassionate', v. 4). Whether we are men or women, the wisdom of God invites each of us to fullness of life through the creative blossoming of *all* our God-given capacities.

Reflection

'Do not be conformed to this world, but be transformed by the renewing of your minds, so that you may discern what is the will of God'
(Romans 12:2).

BARBARA MOSSE

The BRF

Magazine

The Managing Editor writes…   138

Introducing Foundations21   139
Richard Fisher

Barnabas RE Days   142
Jane Butcher

Recommended reading   144

An extract from *When You Pray*   147
Joanna Collicutt

Order Forms

Supporting BRF's Ministry   151
BRF Ministry Appeal Response Form   152
BRF Publications   153
Subscriptions   155

The Managing Editor writes...

'You have reached your destination.' These are perhaps some of the most comforting words we can hear from a recorded voice these days—certainly more welcome than 'Thank you for holding; your call is important to us' or 'Going up' (when you wanted to go down).

In this issue of the BRF Magazine, Jane Butcher describes how, for her and other members of the Barnabas Children's Ministry team, the sat-nav's congratulatory message is just the start of a challenging and fulfilling day's work, bringing the riches of the Bible to schools throughout the country. The team member's 'destination' may be the jumping-off point for a new generation of faith.

You're probably familiar, though, with the saying 'To travel hopefully is a better thing than to arrive' (Robert Louis Stevenson). It's great to reach a destination but, in the Christian walk, the journey itself is our day-to-day experience and continues for a lifetime.

BRF's online discipleship course, Foundations21, takes up this idea, offering four different 'pathways' from which to explore Christianity, and Chief Executive Richard Fisher writes about a new handbook, *Introducing Foundations21*, that explains how the course works. Perhaps you or someone you know needs a top-up of energy for the spiritual journey, a different way of seeing the landscape, or a place to begin their exploration. If so, Foundations21 could be the answer.

Of course, BRF continues to offer inspirational resources in the form of books (in print and, increasingly, for Kindle). As ever, there is a new Lent book for this year, *When You Pray* by Joanna Collicutt, which takes a reflective look at the Lord's Prayer in Luke's Gospel.

In addition, our 'Recommended reading' for this issue focuses on different aspects of love, and the need to travel hopefully in order to find and keep it. Paul's prayer for the Ephesians was that they would 'know the love of Christ that surpasses knowledge [and] be filled with all the fullness of God' (Ephesians 3:19, NRSV). Now that's a destination worth keeping in view!

Lisa Cherrett

Introducing Foundations21

Richard Fisher

What is Foundations21? How does it work? How can it benefit my church? These are the questions we set out to answer in a new handbook for church leaders, published last year.

We're very conscious that church leaders are under tremendous pressure. They face a host of demands on their time and energy, and they're often expected to be all things to all people. We believe that Foundations21 could be of great help to churches and their leaders as they face the challenge of how to help people to grow in their faith and their understanding of God's call on their lives as Christians, and how to live in response to that call—in other words, discipleship. We see Foundations21 as a tool that churches can use in a variety of different ways to suit the needs of different individuals and contexts.

We recognised that most busy church leaders probably don't have the luxury of time to register on Foundations21, browse through the wealth of resources that it offers and reflect on ways in which they might make use of it in their churches. We concluded that we needed to provide something that would communicate the essence of Foundations21 to ministers and lay leaders. So we came up with a short handbook (isn't it ironic that, although Foundations21 is entirely online, it still needs paper to point people to it!) that acts as a ready-reference resource. The aim was to explain the background and content of the Foundations21 'approach' and to outline ways in which it might be used within the life of the church.

Introducing Foundations21 was published in February 2012. It outlines our vision for lifelong Christian learning to be accessible to everyone; for discipleship not to be something that we 'do' but something that becomes a way of life; to move away from a traditional 'one-size-fits-all' approach and offer something more flexible.

It unpacks our innovative 'four pathways' approach, enabling everyone to discover their preferred learning style and how each of these styles is linked to a Gospel. Are you a Matthew, Mark, Luke or John-type learner? (Why not go to www.foundations21.net and find out?)

Having outlined the Foundations21 approach, what it provides and how it all works, the handbook goes on to consider in more detail how the resource could be used in particular contexts in the life of the local church—for example, small groups, nurturing new Christians, one-to-one mentoring, preaching. I wonder if any of the following scenarios exist within your own congregation.

New Christians

Sarah and Max have just completed a Christian basics course. Jane has just been confirmed. They've been encouraged to start Foundations21, each accompanied by a more experienced member of the congregation to support and encourage them. Both they and the 'older, wiser' Christians with whom they've been paired in these 'buddy' relationships are enjoying taking these next steps together—and, perhaps to their surprise, the mature Christians are finding that they are learning just as much themselves.

Hungry Christians

John has recently retired and now finally has more time to explore his Christian faith in the way that he's always wanted to. Emma has been a Christian for a while, regularly attending her local church. Recently she's felt a real desire to know more and to go deeper with God. The usual diet of Sunday sermon and midweek group doesn't provide enough for John or Emma. They're hungry to go further and deeper, but they're not ready to do a formal course of study or training.

Disconnected Christians

Peter travels a great deal as part of his job; Sue has a long commute to work; Andrew works shifts that change frequently; Anita has three small children and is constantly juggling priorities and demands; James cares for elderly parents, so is often away at the weekend; Katherine is in the armed forces and never seems to be in one place for very long. For all these reasons, they and many others like them find it difficult to participate actively in the small group life of their church; they may even find it difficult to attend Sunday services on a regular basis.

Foundations21 could be one way to help all of these individuals.

Introducing Foundations21 also includes comments and testimonies from church leaders and individual users who have found Foundations21 to be of value. For example, one minister told us:

I used Foundations 21 to prepare an adult baptism candidate, as she was fairly new to faith. We went through the joining process together and dis-

cussed where she might begin and what rooms she might visit first. We were then able to catch up on what had been useful and what questions she had, the next time we met. I particularly valued using Foundations21 as it gave my candidate the opportunity to set her own agenda for exploring her faith while enabling me to keep pace with her because I had access to the same material. It also meant that she could keep exploring and journeying in her faith with Foundations21 after the baptism.

One of the keys to enabling churches to make the most of what Foundations21 has to offer is to find a Foundations21 'champion'. Consider all the initiatives and programmes that churches run effectively and successfully; it's unlikely that they do so without one or more individuals who have taken responsibility for them, who champion them. They don't happen by themselves! We at BRF are keen to develop and support a network of Foundations21 champions, who in turn can help and encourage individuals and groups in their own church communities as we all explore, learn and grow on our discipleship journey.

Foundations21 user Paula said:

I have now been a member of Foundations21 since November 2006. Initially I was looking for a well-balanced follow-on course from Alpha. Foundations21 certainly fits the bill! However, for me it has been much more than just a course. Yes, it does provide information, but also reflection and inspiration. It has turned out to be a companion on my Christian journey, constantly challenging my opinions and my lifestyle. Every time I return there is more to discover or reconsider. Foundations21 is a fantastic resource and one I hope to use for many years to come.

The Bishop of Oxford has written:

Foundations21 is an inspired and inspiring gift to the churches. This programme is deep and wide. It's flexible and user-friendly. Above all, it gives Christians and enquirers something to bite on, engage with and learn from.'

It's our prayer at BRF that God would use Foundations21 to transform lives and to help people embrace the lifelong challenge of what it means to follow Jesus today.

Do the leaders in your church know about Foundations21? If not, please do encourage them to take a look! Could you be a Foundations21 champion in your church? If so, we'd love to hear from you!

Introducing Foundations21 is available online in PDF form via the website www.foundations21.net (or directly from www.brf.org.uk/pdfs/Introducing_Foundations21.pdf), making it accessible to anyone who is interested, wherever they are in the world.

Barnabas RE Days

Jane Butcher

'You have reached your destination.' It's 8.00 on Wednesday morning and your trusty satnav companion has navigated you safely to the school car park. Next step: unload the car, make your way to Reception in the hope that a warm welcome (and a cup of coffee) will greet you, and thus the day unfolds.

Such is the start of many an RE Day. From this point on, what happens can vary from school to school. We generally find ourselves located in the school hall, which provides enough space for the interactive workshops.

Our team members have a host of different gifts and abilities and will deliver the workshops using their particular skill set, whether that be drama, storytelling, mime, music or dance. Whatever the style or theme, the focus remains the same—that, as adults and children, we journey together, exploring aspects of the Christian faith in a fun, interactive and reflective way.

Generally we will do that through several 45-minute sessions with a group of up to 35 children in each, which could offer the opportunity to work with 280 children and their staff during the day.

By the end of the afternoon, it is not uncommon to feel exhausted, yet motivated and often humbled by a child's comment or observation, which has reminded us that we can learn so much from them. We are often refreshed by the children's openness and honesty. So the day ends: repack the boxes, load the car, turn on the satnav and 'navigate to home'.

One thing that is absolutely clear is that we could not do these days without the freelance team. We are blessed to have such a gifted team who enable us to meet the requests of schools across the UK. The following reflections are from two members of that team. First, we hear from Ken Wylie, who starting leading RE Days about four years ago:

'RE days are full of buzz. I have to give out more than I expect to receive back in terms of energy but I normally come away from a day in a school with a fresh insight into the theme, and smiling over some comment or incident from the day. It is sometimes like being a stand-up comic, needing to deal with anything that might present itself, such as the quickfire comments that children can shoot out, whether they're 4 or 11 years old.

'It is very gratifying to see the excitement of children in the sessions, and their total involvement in a particular story or activity. I feel that, by now, I should not be surprised by their responses as, so often, they have incredibly perceptive views. The downside is that we are only in a school for one day, so I always hope that teachers are able to benefit from hearing their charges expressing themselves in new ways or offering a window into their lives outside school. A real reward comes when we hear about a normally disruptive pupil who has been able to connect with and fully participate in the creative approach that Barnabas in Schools offers.

'In one Year 4 class, looking at the theme "Whose world?", we had explored what Genesis 1 has to say about creation and had worked out that God's perfect world is no longer perfect and it's up to us to do something about it. Coming into the last couple of minutes of my time with them, one girl gave this comment: "It's good that the world isn't perfect, otherwise we would have nothing to dream for."

'No two days are the same, so there is never room for complacency. Of course, the "success" of any day is heavily influenced by the prayers of BRF partners and supporters. Thank you, and please keep praying.'

The following reflection comes from new team member Sean Arberry, who has recently joined us in Cornwall.

'Speaking from my experience over my first few workshops, sometimes children can imagine RE to be dull: obviously, it's not football or *The X-Factor*! But it feels great when you engage them at the first assembly in the morning with something fun, like an interactive telling of "The Rock", and then, through the workshops, see them find out how exciting it all is. One fabulous highlight for me came during a "Who Comes First?" session, when the children played the disciples being called by Jesus for the first time, and posed for a team photo, having all just become winners. This team of disciples was made up from a complete mixture of talents and foibles, yet it changed the world. It was something that the children could easily identify with.'

Your prayers are so important to us—particularly for safe travel. So, to return to Ken's words, 'Thank you, and please keep praying.'

For more information on Barnabas RE Days, please visit: www.barnabasinschools.org.uk.

Recommended reading

The theme of love runs deep through our book selection for the start of this new year. Naomi Starkey explores the search for love that envelops all our lives at one time or another, asking, 'Do we really understand what we are searching for?' Veronica Zundel explores the love between parents and their children and how the outworking of that love reveals God's love for us as his children. From the pages of *Woman Alive* magazine, a new author to BRF tells her story of searching for love through the increasingly popular internet dating sites, and Lucy Moore offers a new series of sessions for Messy Churches with a focus on growing love and happiness within families as they explore together the festivals of the Christian year.

The Recovery of Love
Walking the way to wholeness
Naomi Starkey

The world's hunger for love can be met only in God's never-ending embrace, but, before that hunger can be understood, one question must be pondered and answered: what does the world really want? *The Recovery of Love* begins in an unnamed city, which evokes the stress and demands endemic to life in today's busy, predominantly urban culture. It embodies emptiness and despair. It ends in the same city, but this city now reverberates with a little of the imagery of the city of God, the new Jerusalem. In between, we are taken to explore a curious yet safe place, a mysterious house of many rooms where questions can be asked, experiences shared and the search for healing begun.

At the heart of the story is the meaning of love—on the one hand, our hunger for it and our often weary search to find and secure it, and, on the other hand, God's breathtaking love for us.

Ref: 978 1 84101 892 8, paperback, 160 pages, £6.99
Kindle edition: 978 0 85746 196 4, £6.99

Everything I Know about God, I've Learned from Being a Parent
Veronica Zundel

The Bible tells us that God is 'the Father, from whom every family in heaven and on earth takes its name' (Ephesians 3:15). If earthly families gain their nature from God's parenthood, what might our experience of family tell us about the nature of God? That is the question on which this book focuses.

Veronica Zundel roots her reflections in her journey into and through parenthood, a hard journey that led through infertility, late motherhood and then learning to parent a child with special needs. What she learned along the way—about love and sacrifice, faithfulness and forgiveness—had a profound impact on her understanding of what God feels about us, his most beloved children.

Ref: 978 1 84101 416 6, paperback, 144 pages, £6.99
Kindle edition: 978 0 85746 198 8

Would Like to Meet
The real-life diary of a 30-something Christian woman looking for love
Hopefulgirl

Shares the ups and downs of a 30-something Christian woman, looking for love after the ending of an eight-year relationship (just as she and her partner were seriously planning a future together). She ventures into the world of Christian dating via the internet, and tries to find 'The One' in a context where single women outnumber single men by a massive margin. She debates questions such as 'How easily can "liking" turn into "love"?' 'What about dating/marrying non-Christians?', 'What to do when the biological clock is ticking and nobody seems to "click" with you?' Along the way, she meets and wonders about TinyMan, CrewCutMan, TeacherMan, BeardyMan, TechniMan and HaughtyMan.

Ref: 978 0 85746 152 0, paperback, 160 pages, £6.99
Kindle edition: 978 0 85746 200 8

Messy Church 3
Fifteen sessions for exploring the Christian life with families
Lucy Moore

Fifteen sessions for Messy Churches that focus on the Christian year: Christmas, Easter, Pentecost and Harvest, with a nod to Rogationtide and All Saints' Day. The festival sessions provide the way for churches to create their own Christian basics course, as the festivals help to establish key points of the Christian faith (such as God's creation and ongoing care for the world; Christ's birth, death and resurrection; the coming of the Holy Spirit), giving a chance to reflect on prayer (the Lord's Prayer session) and the Bible ('Light in the dark', or the 'Non-Hallowe'en-but-still-lots-of-fun-dressing-up-and-doing-wacky-things' session). In addition, Lucy includes festivals that, although not exclusively church festivals, are important as they reinforce Christian values—such as Mothering Sunday, Father's Day and Valentine's Day, which examine love, the value at the heart of our faith; and Remembrance Day, which considers service, sacrifice and gratitude.

The sessions also draw on Keith J. White's book *The Growth of Love* (BRF, 2008), which describes five essential elements for child development and the growth of love, elements which are not exclusive to the growth of love in children but can be used as a useful basis for growing love in adults, too. A further influence is *The 8 Secrets of Happiness* (Paul Griffiths and Martin Robinson, Lion Hudson, 2009), which helps families uncover the real meaning of happiness.

Also included in the book is a 'New starts' session about forgiveness, a 'Where we live' session about celebrating our own community, and a 'Journeys' session to expand the concept of community and offer ideas to use with families who are keen to explore faith further.

Ref: 978 0 85746 120 9, paperback, 192 pages, £8.99

To order a copy of any of these books, please turn to the order form on page 153, or visit www.brfonline.org.uk.

An extract from
When You Pray

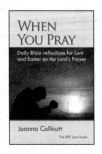

WHEN YOU PRAY

Daily Bible reflections for Lent and Easter on the Lord's Prayer

Joanna Collicutt

The BRF Lent book

In BRF's Lent book for 2013, Joanna Collicutt shows how growing as a Christian is rooted in the prayer Jesus gave us. As we pray the Lord's Prayer, we not only express our relationship with God, we absorb gospel values and are motivated to live them out. Fundamentally, we begin to take on the character of Christ, as we pray to the Father, in union with the Son, through the power of the Spirit. The following extract is taken from the Introduction to the book.

This book is a series of Bible readings for Lent and Holy Week based on the Lord's Prayer as it is given us in Luke's Gospel. It arises from my increasing awareness in recent years that the Lord's Prayer contains all that Christians really need to know; it is the very essence of the gospel. This understanding of the Lord's Prayer is not at all new. It was the practice of the early church to prepare candidates for baptism during Lent by teaching them the Lord's Prayer and using it as the basis for instruction in the faith, sometimes supported by the creeds. In a society where most could not read or did not have access to a Bible, and before the final canon of the New Testament had even been agreed, where disputes about heresies raged, the Lord's Prayer could be held on to as the gift of Christ himself and a distillation of all that the Church understood him to be. Well into the Middle Ages, the Lord's Prayer remained a central framework for preaching and formed the basis of expressions of popular piety, such as mystery plays.

It was wise of those very early Christians to use a prayer rather than a set of statements to prepare people for a life of faith, for faith is not our beliefs about God; it is, rather, the relationship of trust with God that we live out. Learning how to be a Christian is not about academic study in the way we usually understand it. It is fundamentally about prayer, from which the rest of life, including study, flows. This means that, while the Lord's Prayer could be used as a kind of ancient Alpha course manual, there is a lot more to it than that. Praying the Lord's Prayer is an expression of and vehicle for our relationship with God…

Yet recently I have come to recognise that there is yet more to the Lord's Prayer. This has been a gradually dawning awareness. It began with an understanding of the Christian life as one in which we not only follow after Jesus and not only enjoy a relationship with Jesus, but also are somehow incorporated into Jesus. A few years ago, I mentioned this in passing in a book entitled *Meeting Jesus*:

In walking the Christian way we follow [Jesus], remembering the past by walking the way of the cross (Luke 9:23) and looking ahead as we walk in newness of life. Through the Spirit, we also experience him by our side. Most mysterious of all, we find that we are walking into him… (Romans 6:3–11).

This 'walking into' Jesus is a difficult idea to express. It's something about a deep belonging, a kind of identification with Jesus that goes beyond modelling our lives on his. We might want to use the term 'imitation' here. We are used to understanding this as meaning copying something or someone. However, in the Christian tradition the idea of 'imitation' has sometimes been taken further. One of the first and most delightful books I read as a young Christian was *The Imitation of Christ (De Imitatione Christi)*, attributed to the medieval monk Thomas à Kempis. For Thomas, imitation is about following in Christ's footsteps but he also emphasises the direct relationship with Christ that his followers can experience. Thomas stretches the idea of imitation further, talking about Christ as the Way, speaking of walking the Way as a kind of 'entering into Christ' and so taking on a new identity: 'Christ [addressing The Disciple]: My son, you will be able to enter into Me so far as you are prepared to forsake yourself.'

I'd known about this rather strange idea (of being 'in Christ' or 'clothed with Christ' and so on) for a long time, and it had gradually been creeping to the forefront of my mind, but I don't think I fully 'got' it until very recently—St Stephen's Day 2010, to be precise—when I was asked to read the New Testament lesson at the morning service in my local parish church. This was Luke's lengthy account of the life, witness and martyrdom of Stephen from Acts 6 and 7. It is a story that rarely gets a proper airing, among Anglicans at least, as so many of us don't go to church on Boxing Day when his feast is celebrated. I hadn't read it right through in its entirety for ages, and I was unprepared for the effect it would have on me. As I heard myself recount Stephen's assertive denunciation of the religious authorities in Jerusalem and his dying words of forgiveness, I thought, 'How like Jesus!' But then almost instantly this was replaced by another thought: 'No—Stephen is not *like* Jesus; he has kind of *become* Jesus.' As I returned to my seat, my brain began to buzz and into my head popped a familiar phrase—words spoken on the road to Damascus, shortly after Stephen's death, to a young man who had held the coats of his murderers: 'I am Jesus, whom you are persecuting.'

Finally, in my own small Damascus road moment, I started to see what Saul of Tarsus had seen. The young Saul had looked at Stephen and had seen Jesus. The words he heard on the Damascus road confirmed what he already knew in his heart but had been resisting at all costs in his mind: Jesus of Nazareth was alive in his followers. This was not some kind of metaphorical 'living on' but a literal reality. For the voice did not say, as it so easily could have said, 'When you persecute these people it's as if you are persecuting me'; it did not say, 'When you hurt them I feel their pain, for I am in solidarity with them'; it did not say, 'I live on in these people's minds, and when you do violence to them you violate my memory'; it said, 'I am Jesus, whom you are persecuting.' Saul took this statement at face value; Jesus and his followers were one. The rest of Paul's life can be understood as a response to this literal understanding.

> *In praying the Lord's Prayer, human beings take on the character of Christ*

I too have come to an understanding, helped greatly by Paul, and it is centred on the Lord's Prayer. It is simply this: in praying the Lord's Prayer, human beings take on the character of Christ. We don't just act in obedience to Christ or in conformity with Christ, although these, of course, are both true. In some very deep sense, which I hope to explore in this series of biblical reflections, we are incorporated into Christ and are 'in union' with Christ. Lent is, after all, the period in which Christians have traditionally sought to identify more deeply with Christ.

As Paul discovered, this is a transforming work of the Spirit, but it is also a work that is wrought through the medium of words. The words are very important, and the most important of them is *Abba*, for through the work of Christ human beings are offered the possibility of an intimate parental relationship with the divine. Here, at the outset, we find a trinitarian framework: we pray in union with Christ through the power of the Spirit, and our prayer is directed to the Father. Thus we are caught up into the Godhead...

My prayer for those who read this book is that you will have a sense of the great privilege that has been granted to us of holding a precious gem in our hands, of being able to delight in its radiance, play with its many facets, plumb its depths, gain a sense of peace and security from its touch, and in so doing deepen our awareness of our union with Christ.

Luke's version

There are two versions of the Lord's Prayer in the New Testament: Matthew 6:9–15 and Luke 11:2–4. It seems that Matthew's version established itself as the prayer of the church from earliest times. The second-century Christian document known as the *Didache* contains a version which quite closely resembles Matthew's but adds, 'For yours is the power and the glory' (the doxology). A doxology similar to this is also to be found in some third- and fourth-century manuscripts of Matthew's Gospel. Perhaps it was inadvertently added by copyists who had become used to praying the doxology in their daily devotions. At any rate, this meant that Matthew's version plus the doxology 'For Thine is the kingdom, the power and the glory, for ever and ever' found its way via the Latin Bible into the English Prayer Book of 1549, based on translations by William Tyndale and Miles Coverdale. This form of the Lord's Prayer became deeply ingrained in the consciousness of the English-speaking world until the rise of secularism towards the end of the 20th century, and is still known and cherished by millions.

Luke's version, on the other hand, has been rather neglected in the prayer of the church, and this is one reason that I have chosen to use it as the basis of these Lenten devotions. We are less familiar with it and so may come to it afresh… While it's possible that Matthew knew Luke's version of the prayer and elaborated it, or that Luke knew Matthew's version and condensed it, it seems most likely that Matthew and Luke simply had access to different Christian communities with different recollections of the precise words of Jesus. Indeed, we shall see that there are traces of the Lord's Prayer in the Gospels of Mark and John, too. The gist is the same, even though the wording differs. There are also, of course, different wordings of Luke 11:2–4 in the various English Bible translations…

In addition to its relative neglect, I have another reason for using Luke's version of the Lord's Prayer: Luke is the author of Acts. It was, after all, Luke's wonderful accounts of the death of Stephen and Saul's encounter with Jesus on the road to Damascus that first drew my attention to the way that the faithful Christian comes not only to resemble Christ but to identify with Christ. I have a deep respect for Luke.

Finally, and perhaps most importantly of all, Luke's version of the Lord's Prayer begins simply with one word: 'Father'. If we are to pray 'by with and in Christ', that is where we must begin.

To order a copy of this book, please turn to the order form on page 153, or visit www.brfonline.org.uk. The book is also available for Kindle.

SUPPORTING BRF'S MINISTRY

As a Christian charity, BRF is involved in seven distinct yet complementary areas.

- **BRF** (www.brf.org.uk) resources adults for their spiritual journey through Bible reading notes, books and Quiet Days. BRF also provides the infrastructure that supports our other specialist ministries.
- **Foundations21** (www.foundations21.net) provides flexible and innovative ways for individuals and groups to explore their Christian faith and discipleship through a multimedia internet-based resource.
- **Messy Church** (www.messychurch.org.uk), led by Lucy Moore, enables churches all over the UK (and increasingly abroad) to reach children and adults beyond the fringes of the church.
- **Barnabas in Churches** (www.barnabasinchurches.org.uk) helps churches to support, resource and develop their children's ministry with the under-11s more effectively .
- **Barnabas in Schools** (www.barnabasinschools.org.uk) enables primary school children and teachers to explore Christianity creatively and bring the Bible alive within RE and Collective Worship.
- **Faith in Homes** (www.faithinhomes.org.uk) supports families to explore and live out the Christian faith at home.
- **Who Let The Dads Out** (www.wholetthedadsout.org) inspires churches to engage with dads and their pre-school children.

At the heart of BRF's ministry is a desire to equip adults and children for Christian living—helping them to read and understand the Bible, explore prayer and grow as disciples of Jesus. We need your help to make an impact on the local church, local schools and the wider community.

- You could support BRF's ministry with a donation or standing order (using the response form overleaf).
- You could consider making a bequest to BRF in your will.
- You could encourage your church to support BRF as part of your church's giving to home mission—perhaps focusing on a specific area of our ministry, or a particular member of our Barnabas team.
- Most important of all, you could support BRF with your prayers.

If you would like to discuss how a specific gift or bequest could be used in the development of our ministry, please phone 01865 319700 or email enquiries@brf.org.uk.

Whatever you can do or give, we thank you for your support.

BRF MINISTRY APPEAL RESPONSE FORM

Name _____

Address _____

_____ Postcode _____

Telephone _____ Email _____

Gift Aid Declaration

❏ I am a UK taxpayer. I want BRF to treat as Gift Aid Donations all donations I make from 6 April 2000 until I notify you otherwise.

Signature _____ Date _____

❏ I would like to support BRF's ministry with a regular donation by standing order

Standing Order – Banker's Order

To the Manager, Name of Bank/Building Society

Address _____

_____ Postcode _____

Sort Code _____ Account Name _____

Account No _____

Please pay Royal Bank of Scotland plc, Drummonds, 49 Charing Cross, London SW1A 2DX (Sort Code 16-00-38), for the account of BRF A/C No. 00774151

The sum of _____ pounds on __/__/__ (insert date) and thereafter the same amount on the same day each month / same day annually (delete as applic.) until further notice.

Signature _____ Date _____

Single donation

❏ I enclose my cheque/credit card/Switch card details for a donation of £5 £10 £25 £50 £100 £250 (other) £ _____ to support BRF's ministry

Card no. ⬚⬚⬚⬚ ⬚⬚⬚⬚ ⬚⬚⬚⬚ ⬚⬚⬚⬚

Expires ⬚⬚ ⬚⬚ Security code ⬚⬚⬚ Issue no. ⬚⬚⬚⬚

Signature _____ Date _____

Please use my donation for ❏ BRF ❏ Foundations21 ❏ Messy Church
❏ Barnabas for Children ❏ Faith in Homes

❏ Please send me information about making a bequest to BRF in my will.

Please detach and send this completed form to: Richard Fisher, BRF, 15 The Chambers, Vineyard, Abingdon OX14 3FE. BRF is a Registered Charity (No.233280)

Please ensure that you complete and send off both sides of this order form.

Please send me the following book(s):

		Quantity	Price	Total
089 9	When You Pray (J. Collicutt)	_____	£7.99	_____
892 8	The Recovery of Love (N. Starkey)	_____	£6.99	_____
152 0	Would Like to Meet (HopefulGirl)	_____	£6.99	_____
416 6	Everything I Know about God... (V. Zundel)	_____	£6.99	_____
798 3	The Way of the Desert (A. Watson)	_____	£7.99	_____
704 4	Jesus Christ—the Alpha & the Omega (N.G. Wright)	_____	£7.99	_____
680 1	Giving It Up (M. Dawn)	_____	£7.99	_____
814 0	Messy Cooks (J. Butcher)	_____	£5.99	_____
049 3	Family Fun for Easter (J. Butcher)	_____	£4.99	_____
061 5	Family Fun for Summer (J. Butcher)	_____	£4.99	_____

Total cost of books £ _____

Donation £ _____

Postage and packing £ _____

TOTAL £ _____

POSTAGE AND PACKING CHARGES				
order value	UK	Europe	Surface	Air Mail
£7.00 & under	£1.25	£3.00	£3.50	£5.50
£7.01–£30.00	£2.25	£5.50	£6.50	£10.00
Over £30.00	free	prices on request		

For more information about new books and special offers, visit www.brfonline.org.uk.

See over for payment details.

All prices are correct at time of going to press, are subject to the prevailing rate of VAT and may be subject to change without prior warning.

PAYMENT DETAILS

WAYS TO ORDER BRF RESOURCES

Christian bookshops: All good Christian bookshops stock BRF publications. For your nearest stockist, please contact BRF.

Telephone: The BRF office is open between 09.15 and 17.30. To place your order, phone 01865 319700; fax 01865 319701.

Web: Visit www.brfonline.org.uk

By post: Please complete the payment details below and send with appropriate payment and completed order form to:

BRF, 15 The Chambers, Vineyard, Abingdon OX14 3FE

Name _____

Address _____

_____ Postcode _____

Telephone _____

Email _____

Total enclosed £ _____ (cheques should be made payable to 'BRF')

Please charge my Visa ❑ Mastercard ❑ Switch card ❑ with £ _____

Card no: ☐☐☐☐ ☐☐☐☐ ☐☐☐☐ ☐☐☐☐

Expires ☐☐☐☐ Security code ☐☐☐

Issue no (Switch only) ☐☐☐☐

Signature (essential if paying by credit/Switch) _____

❑ Please do not send me further information about BRF publications.

BRF is a Registered Charity

NEW DAYLIGHT SUBSCRIPTIONS

Please note our subscription rates 2013–2014. From the May 2013 issue, the new subscription rates will be:

Individual subscriptions covering 3 issues for under 5 copies, payable in advance (including postage and packing):

	UK	SURFACE	AIRMAIL
NEW DAYLIGHT each set of 3 p.a.	£15.00	£21.60	£24.00
NEW DAYLIGHT 3-year sub i.e. 9 issues	£37.80	N/A	N/A
(Not available for Deluxe)			
NEW DAYLIGHT DELUXE each set of 3 p.a.	£18.99	£29.10	£31.50

Group subscriptions covering 3 issues for 5 copies or more, sent to ONE UK address (post free).

NEW DAYLIGHT	£12.00	each set of 3 p.a.
NEW DAYLIGHT DELUXE	£14.97	each set of 3 p.a.

Overseas group subscription rates available on request.
Contact enquiries@brf.org.uk.

Please note that the annual billing period for Group Subscriptions runs from 1 May to 30 April.

Copies of the notes may also be obtained from Christian bookshops:

NEW DAYLIGHT	£4.00 each copy
NEW DAYLIGHT DELUXE	£4.99 each copy

Visit www.biblereadingnotes.org.uk for information about our other Bible reading notes and Apple apps for iPhone and iPod touch.

NEW DAYLIGHT INDIVIDUAL SUBSCRIPTIONS

❏ I would like to take out a subscription myself:

Your name _____

Your address _____

_____ Postcode _____

Tel _____ Email _____

Please send *New Daylight* beginning with the May 2013 / September 2013 / January 2014 issue: (delete as applicable)

(please tick box)	UK	SURFACE	AIR MAIL
NEW DAYLIGHT	❏ £15.00	❏ £21.60	❏ £24.00
NEW DAYLIGHT 3-year sub	❏ £37.80		
NEW DAYLIGHT DELUXE	❏ £18.99	❏ £29.10	❏ £31.50
NEW DAYLIGHT daily email only	❏ £12.00 (UK and overseas)		

Please complete the payment details below and send with appropriate payment to: **BRF, 15 The Chambers, Vineyard, Abingdon OX14 3FE**

Total enclosed £ _____ (cheques should be made payable to 'BRF')

Please charge my Visa ❏ Mastercard ❏ Switch card ❏ with £

Card no: ☐☐☐☐☐☐☐☐☐☐☐☐☐☐☐☐☐☐

Expires ☐☐☐☐ Security code ☐☐☐

Issue no (Switch only) ☐☐☐☐

Signature (essential if paying by card) _____

To set up a direct debit, please also complete the form on page 159 and send it to BRF with this form.

NEW DAYLIGHT GIFT SUBSCRIPTIONS

❏ I would like to give a gift subscription (please provide both names and addresses:

Your name _____

Your address _____

_____ Postcode _____

Tel _____ Email _____

Gift subscription name _____

Gift subscription address _____

_____ Postcode _____

Gift message (20 words max. or include your own gift card for the recipient)

_____

_____

Please send *New Daylight* beginning with the May 2013 / September 2013 / January 2014 issue: (delete as applicable)

(please tick box)	UK	SURFACE	AIR MAIL
NEW DAYLIGHT	❏ £15.00	❏ £21.60	❏ £24.00
NEW DAYLIGHT 3-year sub	❏ £37.80		
NEW DAYLIGHT DELUXE	❏ £18.99	❏ £29.10	❏ £31.50
NEW DAYLIGHT daily email only	❏ £12.00 (UK and overseas)		

Please complete the payment details below and send with appropriate payment to: **BRF, 15 The Chambers, Vineyard, Abingdon OX14 3FE**

Total enclosed £ _____ (cheques should be made payable to 'BRF')

Please charge my Visa ❏ Mastercard ❏ Switch card ❏ with £

Card no: ☐☐☐☐ ☐☐☐☐ ☐☐☐☐ ☐☐☐☐ ☐☐☐☐

Expires ☐☐☐☐ Security code ☐☐☐

Issue no (Switch only) ☐☐☐☐

Signature (essential if paying by card) `_____

To set up a direct debit, please also complete the form on page 159 and send it to BRF with this form.

Now you can pay for your annual subscription to BRF notes using Direct Debit. You need only give your bank details once, and the payment is made automatically every year until you cancel it. If you would like to pay by Direct Debit, please use the form opposite, entering your BRF account number under 'Reference'.

You are fully covered by the Direct Debit Guarantee:

The Direct Debit Guarantee

- This Guarantee is offered by all banks and building societies that accept instructions to pay Direct Debits.
- If there are any changes to the amount, date or frequency of your Direct Debit, The Bible Reading Fellowship will notify you 10 working days in advance of your account being debited or as otherwise agreed. If you request The Bible Reading Fellowship to collect a payment, confirmation of the amount and date will be given to you at the time of the request.
- If an error is made in the payment of your Direct Debit, by The Bible Reading Fellowship or your bank or building society, you are entitled to a full and immediate refund of the amount paid from your bank or building society.
  - – If you receive a refund you are not entitled to, you must pay it back when The Bible Reading Fellowship asks you to.
- You can cancel a Direct Debit at any time by simply contacting your bank or building society. Written confirmation may be required. Please also notify us.

The Bible Reading Fellowship

Instruction to your bank or building society to pay by Direct Debit

Please fill in the whole form using a ballpoint pen and send to The Bible Reading Fellowship, 15 The Chambers, Vineyard, Abingdon OX14 3FE.

Service User Number: | 5 | 5 | 8 | 2 | 2 | 9 |

Name and full postal address of your bank or building society

To: The Manager	Bank/Building Society
Address	
	Postcode

Name(s) of account holder(s)

Branch sort code	Bank/Building Society account number

Reference

Instruction to your Bank/Building Society

Please pay The Bible Reading Fellowship Direct Debits from the account detailed in this instruction, subject to the safeguards assured by the Direct Debit Guarantee.
I understand that this instruction may remain with The Bible Reading Fellowship and, if so, details will be passed electronically to my bank/building society.

Signature(s)
Date

Banks and Building Societies may not accept Direct Debit instructions for some types of account.

This page is intentionally left blank.